Marky

Work Hard

Enjoy life

&

Live Your Dreams

Kim Butt

BUILD WEALTH
Like a SHARK

The authors, editors and publishers are not engaged in rendering legal, tax, accounting, charitable, and financial planning, or similar professional services. The information contained in these materials and in any subsequent support provided is meant to provide general education. While legal, tax, accounting, charitable, and financial planning issues covered in this book have been checked by sources believed to be reliable, some material may be affected by changes in the laws or in the interpretation of such laws since the manuscript for this book was completed. For that reason, the accuracy and completeness of such information and the opinions based thereon are not guaranteed. In addition, national, state and local laws and procedural rules may have a material impact on the general recommendations. As always, consult a professional before taking any action. While all attempts have been made to vet and verify the included information, neither the author nor the publishers assume any responsibility for errors, omissions, falsities, or contradictory interpretation of the subject matter. You purchase these materials on an "As Is" basis, and you assume responsibility for the use of these materials and information.

Copyright © 2020 Retirement Insights. All Rights Reserved.

Duplication, replication, reproduction, reprinting, or copying of these materials—without permission—by any means, including but not limited to digital, electronic, printed, and/or mechanical is strictly prohibited and punishable by state and federal law.

Permission to duplicate, replicate, reproduce, reprint, or copy these materials, in whole or in part, may be granted by contacting *Mastery Media,* in writing, at the address provided below. Specific details, as to how you want to use these materials and in what format, must be included in the written request:

Retirement Insights, LLC
2535 Washington Road, Suite 1120
Pittsburgh, PA 15241
(800)281-1575

Mastery Media Center
2535 Washington Road, Suite 1120
Pittsburgh, PA 15241

Contents

Build Wealth Like a Shark 13
Kevin Harrington

Understanding the Principle of "True Wealth" 23
Joel R. Baker

Forming a Road Map for Your Future 31
Doug Bauerband

Seven Core Principles for Preserving and
Enjoying Wealth 41
Jeff Busbee

How to Live Your Dreams 51
Kenneth V. Byers, Jr.

The Seven Major Financial Blind Spots 59
Dan Carson

Protect and Preserve Your Wealth as You Build It 69
Joseph Catanzarite

Invest Strategically People Matter Most 79
J. Richard Coe

The One Thing You Don't
Want to Have in Retirement 91
Rey Cruz

Run with Those Running Faster Than You! 101
Chad Dishennett

Success to Significance: When you're gone,
what do you *really* want to leave behind? 111
Peter Dobrich

The Worst Retirement Income Strategy That Almost Everyone is Using 125
Navi Dowty

We Don't Know What We Don't Know 137
John P. Dubots

One Retiring Mistake Can Cost A Bundle 147
Sharon Duncan

Don't Miss Your Bucketlist Window 157
Brian Gray & John Goodhue

The One Critical Factor to Retire AND Stay Retired ... 165
Dan Hagler

Create a Clear Path to Purposeful Living 173
Greg Hammond

Live Today for the Future 187
Tim Hansen

Are You Overpaying Taxes to the IRS? 197
Don Harmelin

The 3 Reasons to NEVER Invest in Real Estate 207
Erica Herbst

Top Mistakes Advisors Make and
How to Avoid Them 217
Dan Hunt

The 3 Proven Methods to
Make a Million in a Recession 227
Scott Keffer

Loss vs. Gain 239
William McLaughlin

Does Gratitude Matter?...249
James T. Niemeyer

Procrastination 257
Anthony Roberts

The 1 Thing You Need to Know About Money.............. 267
Mark Sherwin

The Sandbox Doesn't Have to Be a Dirty Place 277
Art Sobczak

The 3 Reasons Your Financial Success Can Still Leave
You With Worries 287
Barry Spencer & Scott Noble

Savvy Women— Taking Control of their Work, their
Wealth and their Worth 297
Marilyn Suey

Avoid Divorce Disasters—
Choose to Thrive Financially.. 313
Amy Wolff

Charity is the Spice of Life...325
Alan Yanowitz

KEVIN HARRINGTON

Build Wealth Like a Shark

·············· **TIPS** ··············

1. Diversify and Multiply—You must have multiple income streams.
2. Curiosity Overload—It pays to be curious.
3. The Dream Team—Teamwork makes the dream work.

·····································

Many know me as the original shark from Shark Tank and as the guy who created the As Seen On TV infomercial. The truth is, I've worn many entrepreneurial hats over the decades. During my career, I've helped launch over 500 products that have generated more than $5 billion in sales worldwide. I've listened to over 50,000 pitches. I've witnessed a broad spectrum of investment opportunities and want to share some of the top tips I've learned along the way.

Now, I can't say for sure that I was born an entrepreneur, but I certainly grew up as one. My father was a bartender in Ohio who later had the good fortune to open his Irish pub. I was 11 when I started working for him, and by the time I hit my teens, I was working 40-hour weeks in his restaurant. This environment gave me the chance to learn from my father, who, to this day, I consider my first mentor.

Later, as I started my first business at 15 years old, sealing driveways in the hot summer sun, I always circled back to the things that I learned from my father—the work ethic, tenacity and lessons. By the time I was in my first year of college, I had built my first million-dollar enterprise.

Over the years, I've had different mentors, each one giving me invaluable advice on business. But to this day, everything that I know and learned about business begins with the very first lesson that my father taught me.

Diversify and Multiply— You must have multiple income streams

Most kids are taught not to put their eggs in one basket; my father taught me not to rely on just one source of income. It's excellent advice either way, but unfortunately, many people aren't doing it.

This lesson applies to everyone, even if you're an entrepreneur. All it takes is for the economy to take a dive like it did in 2008, or for you to lose a few clients, or for a manufacturer or vendor to make a mistake and wreak havoc on your business.

Fortunately, my dad's business did pretty well. He wasn't wealthy in a multimillionaire sense, but he had a lot of success over the years. Later, he expanded into more prominent restaurants, nightclubs, and catering halls, but even then he was always on the lookout for other income streams. He worked 16 hours a day, six days a week, and only had Sundays off. At some point, he became the official distributor of a device called Magic Fingers, and he and I would spend Sundays installing these massage machines in hotel beds that would vibrate you.

His work ethic and the lesson of having multiple income streams are still with me to this day.

In today's age, you've got to be creative. The fact is, if you always do what you've always done, you'll always get what you've already gotten. I always say, build multiple income streams, and build multiple distribution networks.

So, the question now is, how do you get multiple income streams?

Curiosity Overload—It pays to be curious

There are many ways to create wealth. Some have created wealth investing in stocks, while others have had success investing in real estate. Then there are those, like me, who have created wealth investing in companies and building businesses. It all boils down to one thing—and that is to invest. The key to creating multiple income streams is to become an investor.

So where should you invest your money? Well, guess what? Before you invest your hard-earned dollars, you should start by investing your time!

A key component to creating wealth—and growing it—is extreme curiosity! I call it "curiosity overload!"

Remember how my father spent his one day off a week installing massage contraptions called Magic Fingers in hotel beds because he believed in having multiple income streams? That wasn't all. On those Sundays, I remember him poring through a big pile of reading material, looking for new opportunities. I'm talking about The Wall Street Journal, The New York Times, trade journals, new product news for restaurant owners—the works.

That instilled my sense of curiosity overload and, to this day, I still want to know what's going on. I attend trade shows every year and still voraciously read industry publications. I'm always looking to develop multiple income streams.

The bottom line is, you can't become the guru and create wealth by just sitting at home. You can't be lazy. You have to get out there, meet people, attend events, and press the flesh. You have to seek that 'curiosity overload' situation of finding great opportunities and becoming an educated investor.

At this point, you're probably wondering what you should be looking for when it comes to investment vehicles?

I always say try to find ground-floor opportunities. I like to find a problem that's not currently being solved and then figure out a way to create a product or service that uniquely solves that problem.

That's my investment strategy—get educated and find ways to get a better perspective on the industry and the company.

One of the things I like to do before I invest in a company is look at former employees. I do the diligence—talking to some of these people, finding out why people have left, etc. I also check the buying and selling habits of former employees. Let me tell you... I've gotten tremendous information from people that left a company who were allowed to talk about it.

Of course, not everyone has connections or resources to be an advisor or talk with former employees. The key point is to learn as much as you can about your investment opportunities so you can reduce your risk and maximize your chances of success.

So check respected industry publications, participate in online chat rooms and communities, and connect with former employees if you can. Be curious. Before you invest your dollars, you need to invest your time and become educated about any investment vehicle, whether it is stocks, real estate, or a business opportunity.

Just remember... curiosity overload is critical to intelligent investing!

The Dream Team—
Teamwork makes the dream work

Back in the 90's, I had a company that was doing $100 million in sales. We had ten products generating around $2 million a week in sales. One Monday morning, my CFO delivered some terrible news. It turned out that the bank just grabbed $2 million out of the $2.1 million sitting in our account. That was $2 million that we needed for payroll, inventory, and advertising for the week. The money was gone and it was a big problem.

How could this happen? Apparently, there was a clause in the contract as a merchant processor that if they, the bank, see high returns or feel uncomfortable or at risk, they're allowed to grab extra money as security.

At that time, I only had one merchant account for all ten products. Of those ten products, one was having abnormally high returns. The quality coming out of the factory was so bad that people were calling the bank to complain, and so they grabbed the $2 million, almost putting me out of business.

I learned a valuable lesson and quickly realized I needed a Dream Team. Sure, I had a team of people who worked for me, but I was so focused on growing my business that I didn't make time to find a team of specialists proactively. So I brought in a team of experts and we then went through a major restructuring of my companies. Today, I have dozens of LLCs.

Suffice it to say, if you don't have good advice, then you don't have proper planning. Without a good plan in place, you're likely taking unnecessary risks. You need smarter people than you to advise you when it comes to any financial or investment strategy...

You need a Dream Team

First thing's first—you need a knowledgeable tax professional. Unfortunately, about five or six years ago, I discovered that my tax guy wasn't taking advantage of all the opportunities that are available to business owners. I mean, there are a lot of companies that legally pay no tax because they have excellent advisors.

Of course, you also need a good lawyer or legal team. They're the people that are skilled at finding the best ways to ensure that you don't do anything stupid so you keep more of the money you make. Being able to protect yourself from costly mistakes and bad deals is critical when it comes to creating wealth.

Lastly, there's one big mistake that too many people make, and that's not properly planning for retirement. You need a competent financial advisor for that. You need to make sure that you're putting money away for that retirement age because when you get to a certain age, you're just not going to be able to work anymore. A qualified financial advisor will help ensure that you and your family are well taken care of later in life.

The bottom line is, you need a team to handle the day-to-day planning. But most of all, you also need someone to help you plan for the long term.

BONUS: Pitch like a Shark

Whenever I speak at events or do interviews, most people ask me about my experience as an original Shark on the show Shark Tank. In my years at Shark Tank, there's one lesson that really stood out for me, and that's that you should always strive to customize your pitch based on your audience!

You must do your homework before you pitch an investor. If possible, ask about them and what characteristics they look for when it comes to investing.

Once you're ready to do your pitch, I recommend following a simple 3-step formula... Tease, Please, & Seize! I like to call it the "Perfect Pitch."

1. Start with the "Tease"
   The first step to pitching like a Shark is capturing the investor's attention. So you must graphically demonstrate or verbally escalate the problem that your product or services is intended to solve. You want to "Tease" the investor by showing them an attention-getting problem in a way that is understandable and relatable. If the investor isn't aware of the problem or doesn't understand the scope of the problem, they may not invest.

2. Follow with the "Please"
   Now that you've got the investor's attention, it's time to "Please" them with your products or services. Show them how you can solve the problem with your unique solutions in an elegant and efficient manner. You've got to be sure to highlight your solution's amazing benefits using magical transformations, powerful demonstrations, and great testimonials.

3. Finish with the "Seize"
   If you've done a good job with the first 2 steps, the investor should be open to investing in your business. Here's your chance! You did the "Tease,"

you showed the "Please." Now is the time to "Seize!" You've got to "Seize" them with an irresistible offer. Outline your marketing plan to dominate the industry. Introduce them to your Dream Team of advisors, staff, and experts. Show them why you are the right person to trust. Demonstrate how you will scale the business and impact the world. Finally, ask for what you want with confidence!

This is the same process I've taught and used myself to generate over $5 billion in global sales during my career. If it works for a Shark like me, then it will work for you too!

If you want to build wealth like a Shark, you've got to think and act like a Shark. Hopefully, you will take action now by implementing these tips and strategies in your business and in your life!

Kevin Harrington is an original "Shark" on the EMMY® Award TV show, *Shark Tank*. He is also the Inventor of the Infomercial, As Seen On TV Pioneer, Co-Founder of the Electronic Retailers Association (ERA) and Co-Founding board member of the Entrepreneurs' Organization (EO). Kevin has launched over 20 businesses that have grown to over $100 million in sales each. He's been involved in more than a dozen public companies and has launched over 500 products generating more than $5 billion in sales worldwide with iconic brands and celebrities. Kevin has extensive experience in business all over the world, opening distribution outlets in over 100 countries worldwide. His success led Mark Burnett hand-picking Kevin to become an Original Shark on *Shark Tank* where he filmed over 175 segments. A prominent business thought leader, he is often featured and quoted in the *Wall Street Journal, New York Times, USA Today, CNBC, Forbes, Inc., Entrepreneur, Fortune, The Today Show, Good Morning America, CBS Morning News, The View, Squawk Box, Fox Business*, and more.

JOEL R. BAKER

Understanding the Principle of "True Wealth"

"Every affluent father wishes he knew how to give his sons the hardships that make him rich."
—Robert Frost

············ **TIPS** ··············

1. Wealth planning in its proper role is truly Family Leadership — Lee Brower
2. The more you give — the more you will receive.
3. Know and live your ideal life style

Understanding the Principle of "True Wealth"

For the last 45 years, I have had the pleasure to dream with my clients and then work in helping them achieve their dreams. My clients have taught me there is more to wealth than the financial assets. I have learned that True

Wealth includes **Human Assets, Intellectual Assets, Social Assets and Financial Assets**. I have learned not to focus exclusively on Financial Assets solutions and products. My clients have taught me that we should focus equally on the **Human Assets,** enrichment of the family and introduction of systems that capture the family's **Intellectual Assets.** Distinct and advanced proprietary strategies are then employed to help optimize the family's **Financial Assets**, for the further enrichment of the individual health, happiness and will being of each family member.

The four principals of *"True Wealth"* have developed to be:

1. **Human Assets** are those personal qualities and characteristics that enhance the individual health, happiness and well-being of each family member.

2. **Intellectual Assets** consist of the capture and empowerment of life's experiences, both good and bad, and the formal education of each family member.

3. **Social Assets** are those assets placed back into society for the good of all. They include time, experience, taxes and money.

4. **Financial Assets** are those tangible assets that help ensure financial independence, provide for family legacy and enrich political and social involvement.

When I ask a client what the least important asset class is; which one would they be willing to declare "bankrupt" and lose all the assets within, between **Human Assets, Intellectual Assets** and **Financial Assets,** what do they almost always pick? Which one would you pick?

When thinking about it, they would say:

- "I would not want to start all over again in building my family, my relationships, my health, happiness, values, ethics, spirituality, or unique ability"—all the characteristics of **Human Assets**.
- "I would not like to or be able to recreate wisdom, skills, ideas, talents, traditions, systems, alliance, formal education and life experiences (good and bad)"—all characteristics of **Intellectual Assets**.
- With my **Human Assets** and my **Intellectual Assets,** I can always rebuild my **Financial Assets**.

With this information, I asked myself why am I like all the other Financial Advisors, spending all my time focused first and foremost on Financial Assets and creating systems that divide, defer and dump financial wealth on ill-prepared heirs. This method often brings about one of the greatest fears of affluent individuals—having their financial wealth ruin their children.

Understanding True Wealth can help maximize the value for current and future generations. This process focuses on growing, protecting and perpetuating one's **Human**

Assets, Intellectual Assets and ***Financial Wealth***. The process recognizes one's values and beliefs regarding ***True Wealth*** and creates a system for these values to be internalized in the maintenance and availability of financial wealth for the future generations.

In 1994 I learned from my Strategic Coach, Dan Sullivan, about how to identify my "Unique Ability"— what I was really good at and what I like to do. He introduced me to the Kolbe Test online and once I understood my Unique Ability, I learned to focus on it and not on the things that I could hire people, with other Unique Abilities, to take on and do them better than me.

Ten years before, in 1984, I learned a similar process that my client was using for his sons when they entered the 9th grade. My client was in the oil and gas business and has three sons. Using a similar "Unique Ability" identifier, it was determined that one son would be best outdoors, in the dirt. He pursued an education in geology and after he got his master's degree, he went to work for Standard Oil in the Far East, finding oil for 5 years. One son was very good with numbers and accounting. He got his master's in corporate finance. He became a CPA and went to work for a big 8 accounting firm for 5 years. The third son's test suggested that he would be very good managing people and got his master's in corporate management. He got his first job as an executive trainer with a big 3 oil company.

After five years, working for other oil and gas companies, the sons became eligible to work for the family oil and gas companies. They proceeded to guide their family business to be one of the largest Natural Gas and Oil companies in the United States. Their children are going through the same program now.

In the early 70's one of my clients had built one of the top recreational businesses in the world. He has 5 children who grew up working for the company in the summer. They practiced the old way; the oldest son was groomed to run the business, which he did, but was never happy working in an office. The next oldest son had started several different businesses while going to college and would have been the ideal future CEO. However, when he graduated with all these new ideas, my client was not ready to delegate responsibility to the two older sons. The 2nd son ended up moving out of state and started his own business. Since the children never had the opportunity to learn and practice their unique ability at the family business, they gravitated to other financial pursuits and pressured their parents to sell the business. When my client retired he did sell the business and distributed some of the gain to his children. The business continues to be a top recreational business but without a family member as owner. The grandchildren will not have the same financial opportunities as their parents. They have to start all over.

As part of our wealth planning process, we encourage all our clients to have their children and loved ones take the Kolbe test to identify their individual Unique Ability. What a fantastic gift these clients are giving their children- the path to an occupation they can be passionate about.

Overall, this approach; enrichment of Human Assets, Capture of Intellectual Assets and Optimization of Financial Assets are perpetuated through the structure and management provided by a comprehensive concept we call the Family Bank.

The majority of my clients have set up their own Family Legacy Bank for their heirs.

The Bank is set to help each family member in time of opportunity or need. The client defines how family members can excess their Family Legacy Bank. "Opportunity" would include continued education, business opportunity, wedding costs, etc. "Need" would include health issues, emergencies, etc.

The Family Bank is a structure of inter-linked entities combined with drafted documents designed to coincide with your family's "True Wealth" and Optimized Wealth and Legacy Plans. This structure provides choices and helps create an environment in which family stewardship and values transfer can be accomplished.

The J R Baker Process architecture is designed to provide the structure for the enhancement of your Human Assets, the capture and utilization of your Intellectual Assets and the optimization of your Financial Assets to help increase the individual health, happiness and well- being of every family member now and in the future.

Joel R. Baker is the Cofounder of Financial Planning Services, one of the first fee-based financial and estate planning firms in 1971.

Since 1972, Joel has partnered with many of the nation's premier independent financial planning and service firms. "While I have learned a lot from these associations, I feel I have actually learned more from my clients and what is truly important to them and their families. With this client input, a special process has developed over the last fifteen years that has become known as "The J R Baker Process".

Joel is the Founder of Pacific Coast Youth Polo Association. Cofounder and Director of the Mammoth Lakes Foundation. Past Director, Santa Ynez YMCA. Past Director, Solvang Theaterfest. Past Director, California Culinary Foundation. A member of Gold Cuppers and Chairman of the Endowment Fund Committee for the Vikings of Solvang. We have raised two foster sons.

He enjoys the outdoors, especially where he lives in Santa Ynez Valley (California). Joel has played professional polo since 1970 and has enjoyed raising and training many of the horses he currently plays. He has been coaching United States International polo teams, winning the Silver medal in the World Snow Championships in China and the Silver medal in the World Cup in Chile. Joel was fortunate to attend Fort Lewis College in Durango, Colorado, on a skiing scholarship, and he still enjoys the sport immensely.

DOUG BAUERBAND

Forming a Road Map for Your Future

"Look at retirement as a moving on. One journey has ended and another better one is about to begin."

·············· **TIPS** ··············

1. Family and friends: Continue to love and forgive them.
2. Charity: Look to be a blessing to others first.
3. Stay involved/connected: church, organizations, non-profits. Continue to use your gifts that God gave you.

··

In times past, retirement wasn't even a thought. I remember my Grandparents didn't even have any documents. No will, POA or living will. Even if they thought of writing a will, it would have been done on a paper napkin or on one sheet of paper. Their thinking was, "what is left is left." Our forefathers worked hard until they couldn't. Then the spouse or family took care of them. However, many times their money, assets and possessions went to federal, state and inheritance taxes or Medicaid.

Our tax code has long had a list of instruments that can protect one's family or estate. However, like most of the public, they do not take advantage of such instruments. Even when they do, many times they forget to finish the document. How many instances do we read about the wealthy, sports figures, entertainment world or the family down the street where their estate is in complete disarray? Families are suing each other due to the fact that there was no will written. If there was one, the document was never updated, and the money is granted to the wrong person or heirs. There is no mention of who receives the paintings or valuables. A trust that was written, but never funded, or an estate plan that was fully laid out, but never signed or executed.

Sadly today, many of those mistakes continue to be present. We seem to be very busy trying to make our mark on the world and forget what is right in front of us, our family. It's not your fault though. We are all rushing around with taking our kids to sports, recitals, grandkids, graduations and working overtime. Yes, life gets in the way. But if you want to protect what you have worked so hard for over the years, then you need to take time out and not only develop an estate plan but execute it!

The average American adult watches approximately 3.8 hours of TV per day. That's close to 1400 hours per year. Make the time and start the plan.

I have yet to meet someone that did not want to leave a portion of their net worth or legacy to their children, grandchildren or charity. Many of today's parents are searching for ways not to be a burden to their children along with wanting to leave them more than what they received or started out with.

Currently, if you continue to handle your estate planning the old fashion way, you could end up without any estate at all. Though your greatest desire was to leave precious possessions and your wealth to your heirs, they ended up with nothing due to poor planning or no planning. In some cases, not only are estates in disarray, but the estate had to deal with legal battles. Can one assure themselves that they will leave behind a legacy? Is there such a thing where a legacy could be guaranteed? There are many steps to securing a legacy, but these three will start you on your way to a personal road map.

1st step: The key word is *protection*. How does one protect their estate from wealth predators? We all hear about the wealthy business owners and actors on how they had a trust, but never funded it. Wills were in place, but they forgot to change the executor, beneficiaries or designate items to specific family members, or estate plans that were drawn up, but never signed and put into action. For these reasons, several estates can be tied up in courts and many checks were signed for millions of dollars to pay federal and state government taxes and inheritance taxes. If you are one who takes pro-active steps in protecting and updating your estate, you will enjoy having peace through the night sleep. Protection can consist of trusts on your home (find an attorney who is an expert in trusts), irrevocable life insurance trusts (ILIT) to be written on your term (sometimes) and permanent life policies. Depending on which state you live in, you might want a trust on your assets, which depends on your state tax laws. Long term care policies have changed over the years and become more client friendly. The new LTC policies now have a "cash option" that allows you to have anyone take care of you without checking into a facility or hiring a live-in nurse. In order to qualify for the "Partnership Program," you must add the "inflation guard," which the percentage varies in every state. Money Guard and other alternative policies can be used to cover long term health issues as well. However, you want to review all of these options with your advisor before making a decision. Beneficiaries are another area where estates can be lost. There are only three beneficiaries that you can choose from which are: the IRS, heirs and charities. Sadly, most families will keep those beneficiaries in the same order instead of moving the IRS to last. You can leave a legacy to family and charities by forming charitable remainder trusts; CRUT, CRAT and Lead Trusts. As we all remember the saying, "It is better to give than to receive." In the charitable trust, you can give, receive, leave and receive. <u>Give</u> to the charity, <u>receive</u> an income for life, fund a life policy with the income and <u>leave</u> a big impact to your family. You will also <u>receive</u> a tax deduction. Wow! These concepts have been around for decades. Remember, it's best to make your decisions within your estate plan based on facts not theories, such as; an LTC policy costs too much. As my dad used to say, "How will you decide unless you obtain quotes and do your homework?" Instead, think of it this way; what will it cost my estate if I don't explore the options?

2nd step: The key word is *income*. Unless you are employed by a government/state agency, which are pension-driven, most of us must rely on employer sponsor plans for income. How much income do you need or want as guaranteed verses non-guaranteed? You might have to pay more in fees for a portion of your income to be guaranteed. But for that extra fee, you transfer the risk over to an investment/insurance company, which guarantees you a lifetime income while still being in control of your assets. This allows you the freedom to continue walking where you want to walk and enjoy the hobbies you love. There is a TV commercial that states, "I hate annuities and you should too." No one should tell you what to hate just because they hate it. That would be like telling people I hate steak and you should too. There are benefits to red meat over being vegetarian and visa-versa. Just like there are benefits to a few annuities over managed money. Are annuities for everyone? No. Is managed money for everyone? No. In either case, you should weigh the differences, costs and benefits of each product before investing. If a guarantee allows you the peace you want, and you weighed the benefits and costs, then why not invest a portion of your money with that product? The value you received was worth the fee. You could use this saying in whatever you buy, "In the absence of value, price is an issue." There is nothing wrong with having both a guarantee on a portion of your money and having managed money without any guarantees. Both will allow you to receive income and one usually more income than the other. It's your life, enjoy it. Along with income, you should have a reserve account, which is depending on your comfort zone. This account allows you to withdraw cash from your bank anytime you desire or have a need. For some extra income, you could add a Real Estate Investment Trust (REIT) into your portfolio. A REIT allows you to invest in real estate with other investors. The income is in the form of a dividend, which is usually around 6% and paid monthly or quarterly. There are other alternative investments, which might give you a higher or lower dividend. Remember, on any investment, make sure you make the decision based on facts from the prospectuses, company ratings, commissions, management fees and sometimes hidden fees. When you are ready to sign up for social security income, please make sure you not only make an appointment with your local Social Security office, but ask your advisor for assistance. They might be able to guide you through the options with the resources that are available to them.

3rd step: The key word is **legacy** (Big Impact): leaving money, investments, assets, real estate, coins and valuables to your heirs and/or charities. How do you protect all of these? There are several means of leaving big impacts to your family and charities. As I mentioned in step #1, the IRS, federal and state codes allow several ways to protect one's estate. One plan is to take a percentage out of your IRA and fund a charitable remainder Uni-trust (be sure to check on the tax consequences, if any). The income from the charitable trust funds a permanent life policy, which is titled under an ILIT (irrevocable life insurance trust) as the owner. With this plan, you can contribute to your favorite charities, church or alumni. The CRUT allows you to add more than one charity. You can also do this with highly appreciated stock and real estate and pay no capital gains. The asset must be transferred directly to the charity and not sold prior. The donor receives a 5-year tax deduction and leaves a wonderful tax-free life policy to their heirs (Tax-free only if exempt from your estate, which is why the "ILIT" is listed as the owner). Remember back in step #1, "give, receive, leave and receive." What about your home? You can have the attorney draw up a trust on your house. It could be in the form of a 5, 10, 15 or 20-year GRAT, LLC, partnership, or irrevocable trust, just to list a few. It will vary depending on the state you live in. If you explain to the trust attorney that you want to protect your home from wealth predators, then the attorney should know which document to draw up. The document may vary if you are looking for protection and want to reduce estate or inheritance taxes.

In closing, I asked a question in the beginning, "Can one assure themselves that they will leave behind a legacy?" The answer is yes! However, you must make the first move. Sadly, many people in the world try to protect their assets when it's too late. What if one or both of you has a stroke or start to have the onset of Alzheimer's, dementia or Parkinson's? Furthermore, what if you break a hip or leg and need a cane for the rest of your life? These are a couple of examples of the horrible battles that families face and may encounter without any warnings. No one expected any of these issues to arise. Yet, unfortunately, these events have crippled, bankrupt and destroyed families plus their fortunes due to having no estate protection. We all know what the knowns are, which are death and taxes. Start now in protecting your estate against the unknowns! Remember, you're the one who worked hard for many years, brought an invention to life, and risked everything you owned to go after that dream. Why take a chance on letting everything you built up be reduced, destroyed or taken away because you didn't say, "I will make time." Take a week out of watching TV. Take an estate vacation where you only work on preparing your estate, income and multi-generational plan with an advisor. Remember, only you can put this plan in action! It will demonstrate how much you care for your family, business and charities that you are passionate about. Don't let your dreams die with you; create a legacy! "Done beats perfect every time!"

DOUGLAS J. BAUERBAND is a nationally recognized Financial Educator, Author, Speaker and Retirement Planner, whom you may have seen in NBC, ABC, CBS, and FOX network affiliates and *Yahoo Finance, Wall Street Journal's Market Watch, Philadelphia Business Journal, Wall Street Select, New York Business Journal,* and others. Bauerband has been showing business owners, executives and professionals how to avoid the biggest retirement mistakes and more fully enjoy a secure retirement for over three decades. Doug's proprietary approach to financial and retirement planning creates a custom roadmap so that his clients can enjoy more income for life and a greater legacy to their children and grandchildren. He is the Founder and President of G. Douglas Financial Group, an independent wealth planning firm.

JEFF BUSBEE

Seven Core Principles for Preserving and Enjoying Wealth

"We cannot solve our problems
with the same thinking we used
when we created them."
—Albert Einstein

••••••••••••••• TIPS ••••••••••••••

1. Wealth is more than money.
2. Avoiding loss is more valuable than chasing returns.
3. Harness the power of mindset.

••••••••••••••••••••••••••••••••

"Now that we've retired…" The day has finally arrived, and you can think of nothing but all the adventures you have planned, time with the grandkids, and a life of leisure. Then come those creeping little thoughts; "We can afford it, right? Did we plan for everything?"

To make sure you are retirement ready, there are seven core principles to consider. In this chapter we will cover three of them:

1. Wealth is More than Money
2. Avoiding Loss is More Valuable than Chasing Returns
3. Harness the Power of Mindset

1. Wealth is More than Money

How do you define wealth? Is it how much you have in the bank? Is it the total of your investment accounts? Is it the size and value of your home? If your happiness and contentment are tied to your wealth, then it makes sense to have a clear understanding of what makes up your wealth and how you personally define it. Wealth has three dimensions and can be measured in many ways:

- **Financial** — Do you have a predictable, reliable income that covers the basic lifestyle you want? Are strategies in place that protect you from life's uncertainties?

- **Personal** — How will you stay connected to family and close friends? How do you plan to stay healthy: physically, mentally, emotionally and spiritually?

- **Social** — How do you best give your time, talent and money to causes and organizations about which you care deeply?

Finances for What Matters Most: When Max and Judy retired from their careers as corporate executives, they knew one thing; they wanted to stay in their home for as long as possible. Even though it is a large house—much too large for just two people—they love the fact that their children and now grandchildren can all come home every holiday. Their home holds many cherished memories, from building it just the way they liked, to the marks in the kitchen door frame that chronicle every child's growth over the 35 years they have lived there.

When planning for retirement, this desire was at the forefront. Working with their financial advisor, they have peace in knowing that as they age, they have a strategy in place to provide for them as long as they are able stay in their home; and should the time come, to transition into a continuous care community.

Personal Growth, No Matter What Your Age: Carol is fulfilling all her personal dreams in retirement. Though she lost her dear husband, Keith, a couple of years ago, she would not let that stop her from going and growing. Her career and raising children kept her close to home most of her life, so now is her chance to see the world. She wants to pass this love of travel on to the next generation as well; she stays with and cares for the grandchildren while her daughter and son-in-law travel on much enjoyed getaways. She counts it as a win-win for everyone.

When she is home, Carol takes classes at a local college. Among other skills, she has learned bird watching, photography and fly fishing. All of which enhance her love of travel.

Social Impact: Charlie and Linda have been active in the theater community all their adult lives as performers and volunteers. It is something they enjoy together. Now that they have sold their consulting company, they have time to take a larger role in local productions and on governing boards. Because of their professional talents they have been instrumental in leading fund-raising efforts and a capital campaign that resulted in a permanent home for their local theater company.

2. Avoiding Loss is More Valuable than Chasing Returns

All your life you work to retire comfortably and be in a position to enjoy your retirement lifestyle. Up to this point, the emphasis has been to accumulate wealth by advancing in your career, earning more money over time, keeping spending in check, and maximizing savings and investments.

Once you reach retirement, a big change takes place—your paychecks stop coming! What was once a predictable and reliable deposit to your checking account has stopped. Now you need to find a way to withdraw, or decumulate, enough money to support your lifestyle made up of the "got to have's" such as housing, utilities and medical care, as well as the "want to have's" like travel, hobbies and eating out.

During our work and accumulation years, folks typically feel less impacted by investment losses because they often have time to recover from those losses before they need the money. Beginning with the dot-com crash of January 2000, it took the Dow Jones Industrial Average index almost twelve years, to surpass and stay above that earlier high mark. More recently, it took five and a half years, from October 2007 until March 2013, to recover from the Great Recession.[1] Most folks in retirement can't wait that long for their investments to recover from loss, which is why the focus should be on mitigating loss in order to keep enough money in your portfolio to last your lifetime. One method is to consult with a retirement income specialist who understands that different stages of life require different strategies, and also understands the tax implications of each strategy.

An Avoidable Loss:

Sarah and Mark met later in life. Sarah, a corporate executive, had two adult sons from a previous marriage while Mark was a very successful corporate problem solver with no children. When they married, they decided to keep their finances separate. Sarah had saved the maximum into her 401(k) account and managed it herself using the age-based guidelines provided by the company. Mark used the services of big-name stock brokerage company for his investments. Wisely, they sought the services of an estate planning attorney who guided them to update their wills. The plan was that the survivor would receive the house,

---

[1] https://www.macrotrends.net/1319/dow-jones-100-year-historical-chart.

Sarah's 401(k) account would go to her sons and Mark's substantial assets would go to his brothers.

Tragically, Sarah died suddenly of a stroke. Because they had recently updated their wills, Mark believed that the estate probate would proceed smoothly. Mark had a good, caring relationship with Sarah's adult sons. Plus, per her will, all of Sarah's assets were to go into her estate and then to her sons. All the pieces seemed to be properly organized.

Although they had consulted an attorney, Sarah and Mark did not have a coordinated estate plan. Sarah had named her estate as the beneficiary of her 401(k) account, but she was unaware that her 401(k) required a married person's assets to pass to their spouse unless the spouse signed a notarized document approving a different beneficiary. Because of this seemingly small oversight, Sarah's entire 401(k) account, worth over $1.5 million, had to be paid to her husband Mark, rather than to her sons.

The tax loss was substantial. In order for Mark to give the money to Sarah's sons, he had to pay taxes on the 401(k) withdrawal at his top tax bracket, then use part of his estate transfer exemption to gift the money to them. Had Sarah's sons been properly named as the 401(k) beneficiaries, they could have deferred the taxes, paid gradually at their substantially lower tax rate. The oversight caused an unnecessary loss of over $400,000 and put a strain on Mark's relationship with Sarah's sons.

In hindsight, it is easy to see the benefit of working with a financial advisor who is skilled at developing a coordinated lifestyle and legacy plan. Sarah's substantial estate loss was avoidable. There is no prudent investment strategy that would allow Sarah's sons to earn back the taxes lost due to this seemingly small oversight.

3. Harness the Power of Mindset:

"We cannot solve our problems
with the same thinking we used
when we created them."
— Albert Einstein

- Are you open to new ideas?
- Do you see the value in working with a specialist?
- Are you able to make a decision to move forward?

In the first core principle, **Wealth is More than Money**, an open mindset allows one to think outside the box of one's current understanding. The three examples illustrate how an open mindset can expand your understanding of wealth so that you can have more peace about your finances, enjoy your life more fully and positively impact those people and causes about which you care deeply. Max and Judy find joy in hosting family gatherings, Carol is likely in a far-off land right now, and Charlie and Linda are active in their local theater. All of these retirees chose to open their minds to their financial advisor's guidance, and also act on that guidance.

In the second core principle, **Avoiding Loss is More Valuable than Chasing Returns**, we find that Sarah was comfortable with a do-it-yourself management of her investments. The retirement 401(k) strategy seemed simple to understand with fairly low management fees. She was intelligent; however, she wasn't aware of the restrictions in her 401(k) plan. After she retired, Dave and Sarah were wise to seek the help of an estate planning attorney to update their wills. Unfortunately, since their investment beneficiaries were not coordinated with their wills, and proper documentation had not been completed, a major and avoidable loss occurred. Had they taken their planning one step further and worked with a financial advisor, skilled preparing and implementing comprehensive legacy plans with a focus on appropriate tax strategies, Sarah's husband and sons could have had less distress in an already difficult time. Avoiding loss is more achievable through the coordination of asset allocation and preservation strategies than with investment strategies alone.

In the end, no matter how well you understand these core principals, they will only help you when you are willing to take action. Work with a specialist who is well-versed in a broad range of solutions and can help you find the plan that aligns with your personal values. This specialist should help you develop a comprehensive legacy plan with flexible and tax-efficient strategies.

There is still time to enhance your personal situation. Once your coordinated lifestyle and legacy plan is in place, you should be in a much better position to fully live your retirement, preserving and enjoying your wealth, while improving your peace of mind. Start today!

To receive the full special report **"Seven Core Principles for Preserving and Enjoying Wealth"** please contact Jeff Busbee, www.busbeewealthstrategies.com, 319-777-0808.

Securities and Advisory Services offered through Harbour Investments, Inc. Member SIPC. The examples are for illustrative purposes only. Please consult a professional on your particular situation. Any guarantees are based on the claims paying ability of the company.

Jeff Busbee, CFP® is a Financial Educator, Author, Speaker and Wealth Advisor. As the Founder and CEO of Busbee Wealth Strategies, LLC, he and his team help executives, business owners and individuals fully enjoy their hard-earned wealth while preserving it to positively impact their families and the causes they care about deeply.

Jeff is the creator of the *"Improving the Health of Your Wealth"* Process and a speaker at various organizations and foundations, including Kirkwood Community College Foundation and the Cedar Rapids Medical Education Foundation.

He is the past president of the Cedar Rapids Noon Lions Club, where he received their highest award, the Melvin Jones Fellow award. At his church, his leadership includes serving as Elder, Trustee and Board Moderator. Jeff likes to spend his free time biking, fly fishing and traveling with his wife to visit their two sons.

KENNETH V. BYERS, JR.

How to Live Your Dreams

"Work while they sleep, learn while they party, save while they spend, live like they dream."
—Anonymous

• • • • • • • • • • • • • • • **TIPS** • • • • • • • • • • • • • • •

1. Develop a written financial plan
2. Take advantage of Uncle Sam's generosity
3. Pay down debt

• •

Through the years, I've had many people help me achieve financial success and taught me the importance of saving money. My parents encouraged me early in life to work hard and never give up when times may get tough. They grew up during the depression of the 1930s. Neither of them had the opportunity to complete high school, but it did not deter them from working hard and becoming successful. My father started out as a forest ranger and over the years worked his way up to being in charge of all the state parks in Ohio. My mother started as a cook in my local high school cafeteria and later became in charge of all the cafeterias, which included the elementary school, the junior-high school, and the senior high school. They taught my brother and I how to work hard, make money, and the importance of saving it. We both had newspaper routes at the age of 12. Each week after we paid for the newspapers, 80% of what we made we gave to her to save for our college education. We were allowed to keep 20% to spend or save on ourselves. Because of these early lessons I learned, I have been able to live a great life. I was fortunate to get a college scholarship, so the money I saved was available for me. After I graduated from the University of Cincinnati, I was drafted by the New York Giants. After the season, I decided to stay in New York and attend law school. The owner of the Giants, Wellington Mara, was another person who played a significant role in my success. When he heard I was staying in New York in the off season, he asked me what I was going to do. I told him I was going to law school and he said that was a good idea, but I needed a job so I could save the money I made playing football. He said football was not a career and it could end tomorrow. You need to be prepared when it does end, so you should save and invest your salary. When you're no longer playing football, you will also have a job. He introduced me to his financial advisor and I got started in the business I am in today. I learned early in life we all earn a fortune between our first and last paycheck, however the difficulty lies in saving it and keeping it saved. The past 50 years, I have been able to help business owners and their employees save money and invest and live their dreams. What I've also learned, is that there are some principles that one needs to follow.

In order to live your dreams, you need to save money. In order to pay yourself first, you must have a budget based on your income and where you have decided you want to spend your money. You need to build a budget to categorize your expenses, both short-term and long-term. You need to build an emergency fund into your budget. Once you have set your budget, the next step is to decide where to invest the money you are saving. If you decide to pay yourself First, there are four pillars that need to be set up for tax efficient investing. The first pillar where you should invest your money is before tax money. It is money that can be invested in IRA's and 401K plans. This is the only pillar that the government allows you to keep and save money first, before taxes and invest it for your retirement. This is money being invested tax deferred and grows tax deferred. Starting at age 70 and a half you are required to start withdrawing minimum distributions and pay ordinary income taxes on them. This is called RMDs (Required Minimum Distributions) which are based on your age and amount of money you have been able to defer over the years. All the money you withdraw each year is taxed as ordinary income. In addition, when you die, the value of your account is in your estate. Depending on the value of your estate an additional tax may be due. There are several planning techniques that spread the income tax over a longer period of time for those who will inherit the money. It is important for you to do your planning with wills and trusts so your retirement benefits will pass to the proper individuals.

The next pillar is pillar number two. That is where you can invest your after-tax money into stocks, bonds, mutual funds, CDs and real estate. Taxes are paid on this money based upon dividends, capital gains, and interest earned. This is reported on a yearly basis to the Internal Revenue Service. The investments in this pillar are managed on an on-going bases, to minimize any taxes on the sale of stocks, bonds, mutual funds, and other investments in this bucket. It is important to have diversification of your investments and to take advantage of any gains or losses to minimize taxes.

The third pillar you can invest your after-tax money has very few investment choices. One choice is zero-coupon bonds, the other is annuities. These investments can grow tax deferred and many annuities have guarantees that help in utilizing asset allocations among other investment which may be in pillar two, but the real strength is when income is withdrawn. At retirement, there are a few options that can provide you with an income for life or for the life of you and your spouse. Another advantage is the income tax because you're only taxed on the gain over the investment that you made in the annuity which is spread over your lifetime.

The fourth pillar is also using after tax-tax money. The fourth pillar can be invested in Roth IRAs, life insurance, tax-free municipal bonds and 529 plans. After-tax money is invested in these investments and the investment's income can be withdrawn tax-free. The life insurance investment allows a tax-free withdrawal of the cash value for income tax and can be owned outside of your estate, thus eliminating any estate taxes that might be due.

How do you find a financial planner? There's no one best way to find a financial advisor who is a right fit for you. You should do some background checking. Also, financial advisors advise clients on how to best save, invest, and grow their money. They can help you take a specific financial goal, such as readying yourself to buy a house, or saving money for a child's education, or give you a complete overview of your money. Some specialize in retirement or estate planning, while some others consult in a range of financial matters. Don't confused planners with stockbrokers; they are people you call to trade stocks. Financial planners also differ from accountants who can help you lower your tax bill or a person at your local brokerage office urging you to buy mutual funds. Anyone can say they are a financial planner, but that doesn't mean they are a right fit for you. They may have a lot of characters after their names, and have taken a lot of classes to expand the letters. Typically, financial planners earn their living either from commissions or by charging hourly or flat rates for their services. A commission is a fee paid whenever someone buys or sells a stock or other investment. Today, a growing number of financial planners make money only when you pay them a fee for their counsel. These independent financial planners don't get a cut from life insurance or fund companies. You pay them a flat fee, or pay them an hourly fee to help you with your financial goals. You may decide whether you really need a financial planner. You can certainly go it alone when it comes to managing your money, but you could also try to do it yourself when it comes to auto repair. In both areas, doing it yourself is a brilliant idea for some and a flawed plan for many others. Mastering personal finance requires many hours of research and learning besides following what is happening in the world on a day to day bases. For most, it's not worth the time and ongoing effort.

As you get older, busier and it is hoped wealthier, your financial goals and options get more complicated. A financial helper can save you time.

Financial planners can also help you remain disciplined about your financial strategies. They can help you make smart decisions. Procrastination can cause all sorts of money problems or unrealized potential, so it pays to have someone consulting with you to stay on track.

In order to live your dreams, you must find the right fit financial advisor; but to start, you can ask people like you if they can recommend a planner. If possible, you want to find a planner with successful experience advising clients in the same stage of life as you and if you are a business owner, who is in a similar business. Choosing the right financial advisor is vitally important for your financial well-being. This is someone you will trust with your investments, which makes it a high-stakes decision. The following are some additional things to consider when choosing a right fit advisor.

One of the best ways to find a financial advisor is to attend a seminar. Many good financial advisors offer free educational seminars or workshops. By attending one of these, you will get an idea if he is a right fit for you. You will learn from his presentation and how he presents, and you can determine if you like what he says and if it makes sense to you to follow up and see if you would like to hire him to help you put a financial plan together. Once you have determined that he is a right-fit for you, you should do a background check, and if everything looks good, you can then decide to hire him.

KENNETH V. BYERS, Jr., ChFC®, AEP®, CLU® is a nationally-recognized Financial Educator, Author, Speaker, and Business Tax Reduction Consultant, whom you may have seen in NBC, ABC, CBS, and FOX network affiliates and *Wall Street Journal's Wall Street Select, Yahoo Finance, MarketWatch,* and heard as a Featured Guest on WLW and WKRC.

As the Creator of **The Closely-Held Business Playbook,** Ken has been interviewed on Business Icons by Kevin Harrington, Original Shark on ABC TV's **EMMY®** award winning business series, *Shark Tank.* Ken is the Founder and CEO of Ken Byers and Associates, where he and his team have been showing

Successful, closely held business owners how to get money out of their company on a tax preferred basis, so that they can live a freedom lifestyle and reserve, protect and pass on their hard-earned business and personal wealth for over forty years.

DAN CARSON

The Seven Major Financial Blind Spots

"Choose Your Life and
Live Your Choices!"

• • • • • • • • • • • • • • • **TIPS** • • • • • • • • • • • • • • • •

"Know your financial blind spots. Those
known and especially those unknown."

• •

Financial blind spot number one: **Should I hire an expert?**

"I have a successful career, have done well, and retirement is closer than it has ever been. Why do I feel pressured to know and understand the stock market, retirement income planning, and estate planning; all while working so hard to be good at what I do every day?"

It is not your fault.

When asked what the number one financial blind spot is for most people, my response is simply, "realizing that you do *not* have to do this by yourself." Too many of the people I have the privilege of working with report they feel tremendous stress from their retirement lifestyle planning (or lack thereof). To better understand why so many people feel the pressure they do, we need to start by looking at history. There is a logical answer. **It is not your fault!**

In the early 1900s, we saw America's transition from a primarily agricultural to an industrialized nation come to fruition. As America became an industrialized nation, the two words retirement and planning had not been put together at all like we think of them today. Taking their cue from Chancellor Otto von Bismarck and Germany's example (Mercado, n.d.), the US Industrialists realized it was better to retire older workers with a pension and a gold watch and hire younger workers to increase productivity at a lower cost. The first pension plan was started in 1895, and by 1935 more than half of all large employers and government entities began offering this type of retirement plan to retain valuable employees. Most of our parents were taught to go to work for a company, stay there a long time, and the company's pension plan combined with Social Security would provide for their retirement lifestyle.

Enter the 1970s... and the baby boomer effect began taking place. The baby boomer generation was the largest influx of workers graduating from high school and college recorded in US history and with much longer life expectancies than their parents. The industrialist realized that continuing to offer the Defined Benefit Plans (Pensions) as a retirement benefit would create a huge long-term liability for their company profits.

The first government-sponsored, tax-deferred, individually funded retirement plan started in 1976 with the individual retirement account (IRA). At that time, you could contribute $2,000 per year to an IRA, which was to grow tax-deferred in that IRA until you withdrew the money in retirement. The incentive to contribute to this type of retirement plan was that you could make contributions during your working life and when you retired, you would be withdrawing the money in a lower income tax bracket than when you put it in; thereby realizing a tremendous tax savings. **Most of us did not read the fine print**.

The plan mandated "required minimum distributions" (RMDs) annually beginning at age 70.5, at an amount determined by an IRS formula, that would force us to take distributions and pay the income tax associated with that distribution, at tax rate decided by the government at that time. The truth is all tax deferral in retirement plans (401k, 403b, 457, IRA...) **delay the tax *and* the tax calculation** which is determined at the time of withdrawal. **It will be time to "pay the piper."**

A question to ponder... do you believe your personal income tax rate will be lower or higher in retirement than when you had deductions for your children (if applicable), possibly a mortgage, and you were making significantly less money early in your career?

The Revenue Act of 1978 created the rules surrounding our current 401(k) plans and the industrialists saw a windfall for profits. **Gradually and subtly, American workers were forced to become completely responsible for their own retirement planning.** Before that time, the only people who invested in the stock market were people who had extra money to invest, not typically your average middle-class family, even if they had surplus income. After the implementation of the Revenue Act of 1978, the transition started from company-sponsored pension plans to employee-funded 401(k) retirement plans. To ease the blow of change, many companies initially offered employer matching contributions. Now, many of the matching contributions have disappeared. (Cook, 1979)

Before the "**Responsibility Shift**", most Americans had never invested in the US stock market, and now found themselves responsible not only for their own retirement planning but also understanding the risks and nuances of investing in the stock market to reach their retirement goals.

Fast forward to today, the significantly reduced number of companies that still provide pension plans are primarily large nonprofit organizations, insurance companies, and government entities. I believe this is the main reason many people feel the stress they do about this very important area of their life. The industrialists were successful in shifting the retirement planning responsibility from the companies to the employees without most people being aware of the subtle change. **It is not your fault!**

Enough history. **What are your options?** I have found there are three types of people that come to me for help with their retirement planning. Which is most like you?

The first one is "The Financial Do-It-Yourselfer":

The do-it-yourselfer is someone who appreciates the process of learning all things financial. They enjoy watching their accounts and adjusting when necessary. They have a reasonable knowledge of retirement planning, tax efficiency, legacy planning, and risk management. They have invested the time necessary to understand income planning in retirement and feel very confident they can achieve their ideal retirement lifestyle on their own and still leave a legacy.

The second one is "The Financial Collaborator":

The collaborator is someone who has some working knowledge of all things financial. They may have invested in their 401(k) and saved appropriately over their lifetime. They are aware of how much they have saved in relation to how much they will need for their retirement lifestyle but would like a second opinion from an expert to verify. They also understand that as they age, the desire to spend time focusing on their financial circumstances and details will likely decrease, and they see the benefit of having someone else looking over their shoulder as they age.

The third one is "**The Financial Delegator**":

The delegator is someone who has realized that money is nothing more than a tool. While they have saved and invested, it is more important to them to spend time doing the things in life that are the most important to them. Things like loving and spending time with their family and extended family, while pursuing the things they believe they were created to accomplish. They understand that the financial area of their life is a lot like fixing the plumbing. They are smart enough to fix the plumbing themselves but have come to the place where they are convinced it is better to hire a professional to reduce the current stress of a repair and to prevent costly surprises in the future. They either have found or have decided to find someone they know they need, who is competent and confident in the areas of retirement planning. Developing a long-term relationship of trust, they can "delegate" the day to day management of their critical financial decisions and planning. This allows them to spend time doing the things they love. They also realize developing a trust relationship with a "go-to financial firm" is a must, if one spouse is primarily responsible for financial issues. The comfort of knowing the ones *you* have loved and lived with will have someone to assist them during difficult times, which require difficult financial decisions, when you are not there is an absolute must. **This one thing creates a tremendous "sleep factor."**

The good news is, none of the above types are wrong! The bad news is, most people avoid identifying themselves as one of the above three simply because they are so busy.

So … to get to the purpose of this first installation of "The Seven Financial Blind Spots."

Should you hire an expert?

First, understand *It Is Not Your Fault* that you feel stress to become proficient in these financial areas of your life. Most likely you are bombarded daily with modern financial media from every screen and print on how you can "do it yourself" and save money, thus producing a better retirement planning lifestyle for less money.

If you are a "**Financial Do-It-Yourselfer**" because you love this stuff, invest the time and resources to take care of yourself and your family! If you don't truly love it, you may be identifying with the wrong type.

If you identify with either "**The Financial Collaborator**" or "**The Financial Delegator**", invest the time necessary to find a financial advisor that is competent and understands what you are trying to accomplish. Seek to develop a relationship of trust (**we believe that trust is earned, it is not given, it takes time**) with a qualified financial advisor that understands the things that are most important to you as it relates to your financial life. These are the things at which we strive to excel!

Regardless of which type you identify with; I encourage you to review an article to provide an additional reference point from Financial Planning Magazine at: www.financialblindspots.com\financial-blindspots Measuring the value you receive from any financial advisor is key to your success in this endeavor. (Blanchett & Kaplan, 2013)

I hope you found this first installation of "The Seven Financial Blind Spots" easy to read, easy to understand, helpful and encouraging. Our goal as a firm is to create "Gamma" (more money for less actual risk) for everyone we work with! If you would like to review the other six "Financial Blind Spots" go to: www.financialblindspots.com where you can find articles, archives, and resources to help you....

Choose Your Life and Live Your Choices!

P.S. If you are a collaborator or a delegator and want to get started with your successful financial/retirement/estate planning process, you do not have to wait for the next blind spot installation.

Call our office at 864-242-1914 and let us know you are ready to begin *(sometimes, a simple telephone call is life-changing).* You can also email our scheduling assistant, at info@financialblindspots.com and put in the subject line " response" and we will respond quickly to get your initial meeting or telephone call scheduled.

Bibliography

Blanchett, D., & Kaplan, P. D. (2013). Alpha, Beta, and Now... Gamma. *The Journal of Retirement, 1*(2), 29-45. Retrieved 7 /18/ 2019, from https://financialplanning.org.uk/sites/financialplanning.org.uk/files/user/morningstar_gamma.p df

Cook, F. W. (1979). The Revenue Act of 1978 and Employee Compensation. *Compensation & Benefits Review, 11*(1), 22-30. Retrieved 7/ 18/2019, from https://journals.sagepub.com/doi/abs/10.1177/088636877901100103

Mercado, D. (n.d.). *In apparent first, a public pension plan files for bankruptcy.* Retrieved 7/ 18/ 2019, from http://www.pionline.com/article/20120419/REG/120419842/in-apparent-first-a-public- pension-plan-files-for-bankruptcy

Dan Carson, ChFC® is a nationally recognized Financial Educator, Author, Speaker and Retirement Income Specialist. As the Creator of The Financial Security Process, Dan has been interviewed on *Business Icons* by Kevin Harrington, an original Shark on the **EMMY®** Award winning the ABC TV series, *Shark Tank*. As a Chartered Financial Consultant (ChFC) and Founder/CEO of Advanced Planning, Inc, he and his team have been showing hard working business owners, families and individuals how to more fully enjoy retirement since 1988. Besides helping retirees preserve, protect and pass on their hard-earned money, Dan and his wife, Tamma, love spending time with their two grown children, Tyler and Lauren, and their six grandchildren Carlie, Chase, Cree, Leeland, Forrester and Wren.

JOSEPH CATANZARITE

Protect and Preserve Your Wealth as You Build It

"But those woulda-coulda-shouldas all ran away and hid from one little did."
—Shell Silverstein

• • • • • • • • • • • • • • • TIPS • • • • • • • • • • • • • • •

1. Be stubborn about your goals and flexible with your methods.

2. Plan proactively rather than reactively. You'll notice the options are more abundant.

3. Know what you own, why you own it and how you own it.

• •

"I don't know how I'll ever get to the point where I'm financially comfortable and feel the freedom to truly live life. I'm beginning to lose hope," lamented Tom, who owns a successful small business in the Midwest.

As you can imagine, Tom wasn't the first person to share their concern and doubt with me. Tom's dilemma is a lot more common than we think — successful businesspersons who still have concerns about reaching their financial and lifestyle goals. But those goals are often a lot closer than we realize.

Many may believe accumulating meaningful wealth is out of reach, although it is much more common than you might think — at the end of 2016, there were about 10.8 million millionaires in the US, or about ten percent of the population.

Look around you. Sit at a café and watch as people walk by. You probably won't see very many people strolling around wearing top hats or designer evening gowns, and you probably won't see very many Rolls-Royces or Bentleys on the street. Yet, it won't take long before a hundred people have passed by, all ordinary-looking folks wearing blue jeans and tee-shirts and driving Chevrolets, and ten out of those hundred are millionaires.

If you want to be one of them, the first step is to realize that wealth isn't out of reach. But once you realize that, you have to ask yourself two questions: How do I get there, and how do I preserve and grow it once I do?

Wealth Building

The biggest wealth-building myths come from a mindset of separateness — that is, that wealthy people are somehow different from the rest of us and that wealth is always going to be out of reach. But on the other end of the spectrum, perhaps the more dangerous wealth-building myth is that you can achieve it through a few simple, do-it-yourself, one-size-fits-all steps, or by simply saving a little bit every week, sometimes referred to as the "latté factor." Steve explained his strategy this way: "I bank the money I save from not having those daily lattés, dining out and wasting money. I'm still young, if I keep doing that, I'll have a million dollars by the time I retire."

Internet-based advisors and popular radio personalities always like to harp on the latté factor, misleading so many people into basing their entire financial strategy on denying themselves specialty coffee drinks while ignoring the need for a serious growth plan. Denying yourself this simple pleasure and banking the savings isn't going to make you rich. Nor is enjoying that little indulgence on a regular basis going to push you over a financial cliff. If your daily lattés make you happy and you're not spending the rent money on them, then enjoy it.

Those self-proclaimed financial gurus perpetuate the culture of the quick fix with a backwards "Fire, Aim, Ready" mentality, but they don't know your personal situation — and the silver bullet they're selling won't work for most people.

The cost-cutting your way to growth fallacy is evident in the corporate world as well as in personal finance. One of the most spectacular examples of emphasizing cost-cutting over growth was the merger between New York Central and Pennsylvania Railroad, which merged to become Penn Central and two years later filed for bankruptcy protection. Their first mistake was to focus on the bottom line without considering growth. Management focused too much energy on cutting costs, and not enough energy on adapting to new realities. The result was one of the largest bankruptcies in history.

CUTTING EXPENSES ≠ GROWTH

The same thing holds true for your personal financial goals. Keeping costs down is always a good tactic, but you're never going to cost-cut your way to wealth. People are too quick to deploy tactics with no strategy in mind. Every person only has a finite amount of energy — just so much gas in the tank — and focusing all your energy on pinching pennies carries with it a tremendous opportunity cost. When you expend all your energy trying to figure out how to save a nickel, you're missing out on opportunities to earn a dollar.

Be stubborn about your goals but flexible about your methods

You will always encounter people who think they know better than you but be careful who you listen to. Any advice that begins with "I read on the Internet..." or "I heard a radio show that said you should..." should be politely acknowledged and then ignored. If you've taken the time to do your research and come up with a strategy, don't be afraid to stick with it despite exhortations to the contrary from your brother-in-law who listens to a lot of talk radio.

There are countless examples of people who stuck to their vision despite the nay-sayers and achieved great success.

When Howard Schultz, founder of Starbucks, wanted to start a chain of coffeeshops, people counseled him against it. "Howard, you're crazy if you think Americans will go to a café to get expensive coffee drinks." But Schultz stuck to his strategy and created one of the most successful coffeehouse chains in the world — and more than that, he changed the way people think about coffee.

That said, balancing your productive stubbornness with a little flexibility is essential. Circumstances change. They don't make Studebaker automobiles anymore, but it remains one of the best examples in corporate history of the ability to change with the times. The company started making covered wagons in 1830. But as demand for covered wagons began to wane and the automobile became the more popular method of transportation, they became the only wagon maker to successfully make the transition, entering the automobile business in 1902, lasting until the last Studebaker rolled off the assembly line in 1964.

Avoid paralysis by analysis

Software companies work by a "just good enough" strategy of putting out a software product when it's "just good enough," but not perfect. This model has worked well. It allows the product to go to market quickly, while allowing for improvements over time based on market response and user feedback. Software companies could spend years agonizing over just the right strategy, fine-tuning each product to absolute perfection — but doing so would cause them to miss out on opportunities and risk almost certain obsolescence. Your strategy to build wealth should be like the software companies.

Einstein once said, *"Not everything that counts can be counted, and not everything that can be counted, counts."* Too much time spent analyzing minor details that don't matter may cause you to miss a window of opportunity that would otherwise lead to great success.

New ideas, new strategies and good advice

Building wealth requires constantly looking ahead and searching for new opportunities. If you're not happy with your present — or even if you are — the first step in wealth building is to take control of your future, and to realize that even if the status quo works for you right now, it may not always be so.

Here's the good news...building wealth doesn't always have to come from sophisticated investments, it may come from something as simple as a second career or an unexpected opportunity. As we saw earlier, true wealth creation doesn't come from cutting costs and self-denial. Rather than figuring out how to divvy up a small pie so everything is covered, create a strategy to get yourself a bigger pie.

If advancement possibilities in your current workplace are limited, then it's time to look at other ways to generate an income. The "gig economy" has delivered enormous opportunities for those who want a second income, or even an opportunity to build a new business. But before we talk about the gig economy, we must define it. On the low end of the gig economy, we see Uber drivers and grocery delivery services, but we sometimes forget there is a high end to the gig economy as well. More specialists, experts, consultants and even high-level executives are renting out their services on their own terms, and for high-dollar figures, and a closer look at these opportunities may present you with a venue for expanding your income and providing you with additional wealth to save or invest.

Building wealth seldom involves sticking with the same strategy, even if it happens to be working in the present. Continuing to do the same thing, day in and day out, seldom yields significant improvements — be open to changing your methods, your strategy, and even your entire career.

Wealth Protection

I've met far too many people who worked hard to accumulate wealth only to have their circumstances change unexpectedly and rapidly. We live in a fast-changing world, and having wealth now is no guarantee of having it in the future. Building wealth seems like a tall mountain to climb but typically is the less challenging part of the equation — keeping it once you've built it often is the larger challenge.

Superficial articles on wealth often revolve around simplistic, one-size-fits-all tactics which don't reflect your personal situation. A better approach is to start with your vision of the ideal ... your personal Norman Rockwell. Your strategy needs to be centered on the lifestyle you want to have and legacy you want to leave. Important steps include:

- Assess your current tax situation. Opportunities and benefits may exist.
- Understand who inherits your assets when you die and how it's distributed.
- Know what you own and how it's titled.
- Understand the risks that exist and how to manage them.

There have been 20 major changes to the tax code in the last 10 years. Understanding how those changes can impact you and how you can benefit from them is paramount. And don't forget that there will be change after change throughout the rest of your lifetime so be prepared to pivot when the time comes.

A question I've asked a countless number of people is, "Do you know how much money you have and where it's going when you die?" How much is going to the big three beneficiaries: Family, charity, IRS? The resounding answer is "I don't know." This answer is different for everyone because the wealth you accumulated, and your personal vision need to be re-assessed constantly to determine your top risks in each planning area.

Build it, grow it, and protect it

Building, growing and protecting wealth requires constant vigilance, the ability to change and adapt, and having a clear vision. Who you listen to will inform your strategy and ultimately, its success. Be selective about who you listen to. Everybody likes to give advice, but few provide guidance that will be right for you. It's important to have a vision of what you want to accomplish. The vision you create should then become your mission, your driving force, part of who you are.

- Think big. Don't start by saying "If I only had more money, I would ..." Start with your ideal goal, and then work backwards to figure out how to achieve it.
- Don't limit your strategy to cost-cutting only. Focus on growth.
- Turn down the noise. Everyone wants to tell you how to manage your money, but very few people are qualified to do so.
- Don't be a do-it-yourselfer. You've worked hard to build wealth. Hire the necessary specialists to make sure you're able to grow your wealth, and preserve, protect, and pass it on.
- Create a vision of your ideal lifestyle and legacy. But don't stop with visualizing — picturing it in your mind won't make it so. Take action to make it happen.

How will you get there? We are fortunate to be living in a time where opportunities abound. Advanced technology, telecommunications tools and gig platforms have made it possible to engage in new wealth-building tactics that were never before possible. With the right tools and the right guidance, your desired level of wealth is well within reach.

JOSEPH CATANZARITE, CFP® is a recognized **Financial Educator, Author, Speaker** and **Retirement Planner.** He is the Co-Author of *Retire Abundantly: The Proven Principles To Create A Worry Free Retirement With Less Stress,* who shows managers, executives and business owners how to build and preserve their hard-earned wealth through tax smart planning. Joe is on a mission to show clients how to "live fully in the moment and be fully prepared for the future." Joe graduated from St Joseph College in 2003 with a Bachelor's Degree in finance. He attained his Certified Financial Planner certification in 2010. Joe has been helping business owners, professionals and families for over 13 years. Joe and his wife, Katie, have three children, Cecilia, Rocco and Malia.

J. RICHARD COE

Invest Strategically
People Matter Most

> "Take away my factories but leave my people and soon we will have a new and better factory."
> —Andrew Carnegie

••••••••••••• **TIPS** ••••••••••••••

1. Invest longer.
2. Invest wider.
3. Invest deeper.

••••••••••••••••••••••••••••••••••

Why Invest?

Today and tomorrow compete with each other. It is not easy to defer consumption. Think of the many ways you can spend your time and money.

Our world is rapidly changing in mind-boggling ways. No one really knows what our world will be like in five or ten years, let alone twenty or thirty years?

Will you be ready for what lies ahead?

When you invest you are voting for your future and the future of those you love.

What Are You Trying To Accomplish?

What is the most effective way to position yourself for the future?

In his highly acclaimed #1 nationwide bestseller *The 7 Habits of Highly Effective People* Stephen Covey stressed the importance of beginning with the end in mind. It takes work to reflect on and process what matters most to you.

Many of us once had the capacity to dream about our future. Some of us had encouragement in this while others of us were largely on our own. For many people at or near retirement, it can be difficult to really open their minds and dream about the future. Many people seem to function on auto pilot. Yet often there is a need to think more about the possibilities.

What percentage of Americans have clarity regarding their purpose in life? The more clearly you see your life purpose, the more likely you are to make wise choices as to how you use your money, time, and energy.

We all need help. The prudent among us acknowledge need for help. You may be recognizing your need for assistance by reading this book.

To a large extent, you have the answers for your future within yourself. But you need the help of others to draw out those insights and discover your dreams and your concerns. You will make better decisions if you have trusted advisors or friends who ask the right questions and listen attentively with respect and appreciation for you.

Embrace the premise that your wealth is more than money. Your future can be thought of in terms of you, your faith, your relationships, your circumstances, and your possessions. It is never too late to see things a little differently or even change our minds. Imagine having a well-grounded sense of purpose that resonates deeply with you and that you are willing to share with trusted family members and friends. This will take time and require the input of others. As you are increasingly mindful of what matters most to you, you will approach those important investment decisions relating to money, time and energy with more confidence.

You are probably familiar with the concept of compounding. Some refer to it as the eighth wonder of the world. Better tomorrows can flow from thoughtful decisions today.

Having been a CERTIFIED FINANCIAL PLANNER™ professional since 1983 and having had the privilege of being a trusted advisor to conscientious people, I can make some observations. You want financial security. You want financial freedom. You want to be able to maintain or perhaps even improve your lifestyle. You want to be able to do and accomplish what matters most to you. At the deepest level, perhaps you want to have an impact on your family, your friends, or causes that are important to you. Your investment choices are consequential.

We embrace the pyramid of clarity. It starts with your vision. You build on that with your priorities and then your specific goals. Then a plan can be established, and specific, important investment choices can be made. Yes, it is a process. Our proprietary process to help people in this manner is *The Abundant Wealth Process*.

How Can You Invest More Wisely?

Here are three tips that can help you become a smarter investor:

1. Invest longer.
2. Invest wider.
3. Invest deeper.

Invest Longer

Preoccupation with short-term market movements can sabotage your results. My biggest personal investment mistakes have been selling too soon.

Stock market corrections have some similarity to sore throats or common colds. They are unpleasant, but not dangerous. Usually it is only a matter of months before the correction is history. Living with correction bounces will often prove wiser than making defensive moves. Bear markets, typically linked with recessions, are different. They are serious, more like cancer. It may take four to six years to recover from a bear market. For those who are withdrawing money during a bear market, they may never recover financially from the devastation of a bear market.

Apple became the most valuable company in the world, but that was after coming close to failure. Amazon invested huge amounts in infrastructure and gaining market share before realizing great profit. While there may be such a thing as overnight success, typically it takes considerable time for investments to produce attractive results.

You may know of people who have gone through a lot of money. Perhaps you know of people who have left too much or too little to their family. You can think of your wealth as two sides of a coin—lifestyle and legacy. Either way, a long-term perspective produces benefits.

Invest Wider

Many people learn about risk the painful way—they get burned. While investors can over-react to risk and be paralyzed, a better approach is to seek to understand and manage risk. To a large extent, risk management is the key to better outcomes.

Much could be said about risk. While there are different ways to understand, evaluate and measure risk, there are key questions that should be considered:

1. How much risk do you need to take?
2. How much risk are you willing to take?
3. How much risk are you actually taking?
4. Are you being compensated properly for the risk you are taking?

There are not many true principles of finance, but one of those is the importance of diversification. Risk management is vital, and diversification reduces risk.

Wisdom is reflected in that old saying, "Don't put all of your eggs in one basket." There is benefit from investing in different types of assets, whether financial assets such as stocks and bonds or physical assets such as real estate. It is important to diversify not only between what are known as asset classes, but within an asset class such as stocks.

Risk can be reduced by having some of your money in relatively safe investments. Risk can also be reduced by intentional defensive moves. Whether you reduce risk by use of relatively safe investments or through intentional defensive moves, you typically pay a price. By limiting the bounces, you limit the gains when stocks are doing well. If you make intentional defensive moves, you will sometimes get whipsawed and pay a price. Specifically, you may sell at one price and pay more later to get the equivalent.

There is a saying in sports — "Offense wins games, but defense wins championships." How much defense do you want and how do you want to accomplish it? The fact that defense can be costly does not mean you should not have a good defense. As Tom Halvorson and I communicate in our book *Transformational Investing,* a reliable defense can be a game changer!

You can invest to address future needs or future desires. Ideally, your needs would be addressed in ways that provide security. You may be willing to take more risk as it relates to your desires.

Invest Deeper

Can You Find A Better Investment Than Yourself?

Those who accomplish much with their lives have typically invested much in themselves. Most of us can only imagine what kind of commitment it takes to become an Olympic athlete or a professional athlete. One person decides to be a teacher. An investment is required. Another person wants to be the best teacher he or she can be. An even greater, on-going investment is required. While the training or education may be formal or informal, most people have to invest in themselves if they want remarkable results.

As a person, you are of incalculable value. In view of that, can you find a better investment than yourself? You live in a world with a vast range of opportunities. You have unique inclinations, abilities, and interests. There are wonderful profiling tools available today to help us learn how we are made. The better we understand who we are, our strengths, our aptitudes, our potential, the more wisely we can invest in ourselves. Close friends who know us well can hold a mirror in front of us and help us understand ourselves better. Our spouses can also help us see ourselves more clearly.

We probably first think of coaches in the context of sports. Many coaches provide so much value that they are extremely well paid. The best athletes have benefitted immensely from their coaches. A smart investment in your future might be a piano teacher, an art instructor, a business coach, a personal trainer, a life coach, or someone with experience or authority in a realm important to you.

From both a personal and professional perspective, I have invested in myself for decades. My investments in my business coach and my personal trainer require money, time and energy.

You may want to invest deep by investing in your own business. That typically means investing both in yourself and in others.

What About Investing in Others?

If you accept the premise that human beings are eternal beings, what would be better than investing in people? My belief is that the best investment we can make in others is to love them. There is inestimable value in investing in others.

I am very grateful for people who have invested in me. First, I think of my parents. I also think especially of my first-grade teacher who taught me to read and my fifth-grade teacher who taught me to write.

Having experienced deep and wide benefits from people who have invested in me such as parents, family, friends, teachers, colleagues, bosses, authors, coaches and pastors, I have wanted to invest in others.

Recently I asked about 10 men in their 20s, "Which is more difficult to achieve—relational success or financial success?" All of them answered, "Relational success." There are millions of Americans who have achieved a high degree of financial success. How many Americans have achieved a high degree of relational success? Would you agree that relational success is a more worthwhile goal than financial success, and, for many people, more difficult to accomplish?

Would you agree that people matter more than money, and that money is best thought of as a tool, rather than as an end in itself?

Conclusions

If you are like most people, you can do more that matters. Take time to reflect on what really matters to you. What would you do if you had good health but knew you had only 3 more years to live on this earth? If you live for many more years and want to look back with gratitude on how you have invested your money, time, and energy, what should you be doing now? What would you want someone to say about you and your choices at your funeral?

Opportunities abound. You can improve your future by making prudent investments today. By investing in financial instruments or physical assets such as real estate you can have more security and more freedom and perhaps give more to people and causes which are important to you.

By investing in yourself you can be more productive and have more enjoyment in the years ahead. You will be able to make better use of what you have, whether it is money, time, or energy. By investing in others, you can have more fulfilling relationships.

Your better future may start with a personal, customized plan. You can learn more about *The Abundant Wealth Process* at www.CoeFinancialServices.com.

As the founder of Coe Financial Services and a CERTIFIED FINANCIAL PLANNER™ professional since 1983, **Richard Coe** has gone through life learning and passing on what he has learned to others.

Richard started investing in stocks with money earned from mowing lawns and shoveling snow while in middle school. Owning part of a big company was fascinating to him. Since then he has embraced the idea of making money with money by owning shares of large companies. More significantly, he has invested substantially in himself through formal and informal education and nationally prominent coaches. Today, Richard is better positioned than ever to help people. Richard is a financial educator and speaker. He is the co-author of Transformational Investing and the creator of The Abundant Wealth Process. He has an MBA in Finance and Accounting from Chicago Booth.

REY CRUZ

The One Thing You Don't Want to Have in Retirement

Imagine being seven and a half years old, going to second grade with your legs and feet so pigeon-toed, that your big toes on each foot are practically touching each other. In the 60's, the way they fixed it, was to put a big brown belt around your waist with cable going down your legs which attached to "Forest Gump" boots. You look like the "Terminator," but you are not as cool and invincible as him. In addition to the hardware you are wearing to fix your lower body, you do not speak English. That's how I entered the second grade. My seven and eight-year-old classmates were brutally honest and treated me differently. But there was one teacher, Ms. Johnson, who always kept the kids away, didn't let them pick on me, tease me, and didn't let them verbally abuse me. She protected me, hugged me, and told me that it was going to be ok. Since going to second grade I have always hated bullies.

I grew up in a military family. My dad is from a poor family of eight siblings from the country of Puerto Rico. At 18, he joined the US Army as a recruit and after 29 years he retired as a Sergeant Major. My dad served in Korea during non-war time and two tours in Vietnam, along with being a drill sergeant. When my dad assigned you a task, you did it, you did it immediately, and you did it to the best of your abilities. After the task was completed, you prepared for inspection and if it wasn't done to his standards, you did it again. As the oldest of three boys in our family, I got the brunt of that upbringing. My motto to this day is, "Do Things Better Than Expected."

My mother met my father in the country of Panama when he was stationed in the Canal Zone; this was when the US still owned the Canal Zone. My mother taught me from a very young age to help people. She was always volunteering, either in the church groups that we attended in the many military bases we traveled to and from or even in the officer wife groups helping different transferred officer families get acclimated to the base. There was always a person or a family that needed some kind of help. We did not have many material possessions in our house. If you were in need, my mom went out of her way to make sure that you always got a present on either Christmas or your birthday. Usually, we would go to different garage sales to find little trinkets or gifts that my mom always kept track of in the back of her mind that different people needed. Sometimes we could not find a perfect gift for someone but even if it was something as small of a gift as 25 cents, she understood that receiving a gift was special and could make someone happy.

February 14th, 2020 celebrates my being in the investment advisory business for 35 years. In those 35 years, we have helped over 350 families in the western suburbs of Chicago with their overall financial plans. Our firm has been blessed; I get to help amazing families! In addition, due to our blessings, I have been able to do many things I never dreamed of writing books, traveling, achieving Certified Financial Planner practitioner status, having my own radio presence in Chicago, appearing on TV, teaching classes at local libraries and colleges and public speaking.

During my 35 years, I have received many questions from clients and non-clients like, "What's the best stock or investment?" or "What is the market going to do?" One of the things I learned early in my career is that no one knows what an individual investment or the whole stock market is going to do! Having said that, we have put together holistic financial plans with our 9 Step "Cruzing Into Retirement" process for hundreds of families which provides those families confidence, peace of mind, and the best tactics & strategies for their specific situations.

We specialize in helping clients 50 years of age and older, to have a written Retirement Income Plan. We truly believe that you must have all of your income documented, projected, and in a *written document* to achieve a comfortable and confident retirement. In the words of Edward Deming: "In God We Trust, everyone else bring Data." (Google him.)

You must see your retirement income numbers using mathematics to verify and understand your true situation.

There are many financial advisors that are excellent in the accumulation of dollars for retirement, that do not have the necessary skills for creating a Retirement Income Plan. Withdrawing from retirement investments, reviewing a current tax liability and an overall tax reduction strategy are necessary for a peace of mind retirement plan. Accumulation of the dollars for retirement is only one step and sometimes you just outgrow your advisor. Twice as many people die going down Mt Everest as do going up! Do not let that happen to your Retirement Income Plan. We have income and expense worksheets on our website to allow clients to start to put their numbers together going into retirement. We know from Employee Benefit Research Institute that 64% of workers are very or somewhat confident that they will have enough money to live through retirement. But only 38% of workers or their spouses have actually tried to calculate their numbers.

I have learned many things as I became a Certified Financial Planner, a securities representative and a RIA, Registered Investment Advisor. When it comes to the investment world, there are many systems that you can use to grow your money. You can buy and hold, you can use Value Line, you can use Investor's Business Daily Can Slim system, or you can use Modern Portfolio Theory. A well designed Modern Portfolio Theory plan can get you thru all market conditions. In addition, having a Principal Protection Program can allow you to continue to have cash-flow when the stock market goes against us and many of our accounts are down. The sequence of returns can negatively affect your portfolio in the early years of your retirement if the market goes down like it did in 2000, 2001, and 2002.

We prefer to use Modern Portfolio Theory because of its discipline and non-emotional decisions that are made with a portfolio. There are 4 very important things in Modern Portfolio Theory that you must understand and utilize:

- First: What is your risk tolerance?
- Second: What asset classes should you be in?
- Third: What percentage should you have in those asset classes?
- Fourth: How should you rebalance your portfolio?

This type of disciplined system can help an individual and their family get through all sorts of market conditions. We have a complimentary tool on our website, www.ReyCruz.com, called "Does My Portfolio Fit Me?" which in 8 minutes or less can assess your risk tolerance. You can use it with no obligation. Modern Portfolio Theory was conceived by Harry Markowitz in 1952, a professor at the University of Chicago, where he received a Nobel Prize for his financial work on MPT. Eugene Fama, also won the Nobel Prize, and is considered the modern day "Father of Finance." Modern Portfolio Theory is widely used throughout the country with DFA advisors.

Your investment plan and choices based on your risk tolerance are only one step in our 9-step process. You also have to evaluate your Risk Management and Asset Protection. When you go into retirement, the need for life insurance needs to be re-evaluated. You may no longer need the life insurance for the death benefit like in the early years of life, that would have paid off your home, your car, children college funds and other liabilities. Your life insurance now needs to be evaluated to be able to provide your life insurance *and* long-term care benefits. 70% of households will need some sort of long-term care coverage after the age of 60. Many advisors will grow a nice portfolio of $500,000, as an example, for you, but if you need four years of long-term care and spend down $400,000 of that portfolio, you leave your spouse with only $100,000 left to live on.

There are 7 ways to take care of the long-term care problem that many retirees will have, and many people do not understand that Medicare benefits only pay for skilled nursing care and nothing else for long term care. If you cannot do 2 activities of daily living, which are eating, bathing, dressing, using the restroom, moving from place to place, and continence; you are considered to need long term care. This is an area that, if not covered in your retirement plan, can leave your spouse or beneficiary left with little to none of the assets you accumulated in your lifetime. Most investment brokers will not deal with this liability or provide solutions.

What's The Point?

1. No one knows what the Stock Market will do.
2. Have a Comprehensive Financial Plan.
3. Get a Written Retirement Income Plan.
4. Develop a Discipline Stock Market Strategy.

5. Evaluate your Risk Tolerance.
6. Principal Protection Program helps for income, in down markets.
7. A Long-Term Care incident can destroy your portfolio.
8. Sometimes you outgrow your advisor.

35 years of being a financial professional has taught me many things, but today I want to help you with THE MOST IMPORTANT OF ALL FINANCIAL RECOMMENDATIONS. Very few financial experts are talking about it and many tax experts are getting it wrong! There are very few financial deadlines that people have except the dreaded April 15th tax deadline. But by April 15th most of the tax planning that you can do for the previous tax year is long gone.

There are two tax liabilities that most taxpayers never plan for: this year's tax reduction strategies and their overall tax liability with all of your tax deferred investments. I want to explain to you the plan that many of you are on and you have no idea that it's coming. This is all about reducing your family's overall tax liability with your deferred accounts. As a member of Ed Slott's, Master Elite IRA Advisor study group for 14 years, I have studied what happens to consumers with their largest accounts. www.IRAHELP.com

Ask yourself this question...if you have $1,000,000 in an IRA/401k/403B TSA/457/ ESOP account, on which you got a past year tax deduction, you will, under current law, start to have withdrawal of your RMD, required minimum distribution, by age 72. 100% of that RMD will be taxable at ordinary income taxes which is your highest tax rate. If you do not take out that distribution or calculate the amount wrong, there is a 50 % penalty. Under current tax law there are opportunities to reduce your overall tax liability before you get to age 72. Tax rates have never been lower and the brackets on how much you can make have currently gotten larger.

Let me give a small example with easy to understand numbers... let's say you make $100,000 a year and you contribute $10,000 into a tax-deductible retirement plan. Based on a married person filing jointly and using the standard deduction, you will save 12% of tax on that money that is contributed. You will save approximately $1,200 in tax per year, now let's say you will do that for 30 years, $1,200 x 30 years, equal $36,000 total tax savings. Now if you let that $10,000 grow every year for 30 years at 7% interest, annual deposits and that turns into a nice amount of $1,020,920. (calculated on www.Dinkytown. com). To recap ... you got a $36,000 tax deduction benefit and now you have a $1,020,920 taxable account. Is that small of a tax deduction worth having a million dollar fully taxable account? When we run the numbers for many people it is not.

Everyone is telling you to deposit money in these accounts and get the small tax deduction NOW! I'm telling you that if you're going into retirement with large amounts of money in these taxable accounts, there are many landmines that will blow up your retirement accounts at different steps that no one is advising you about. In addition, when you take money out of these accounts many of you may pay additional taxes on your social security income, increased fees on Medicare premiums and a possible extra tax to pay for Obamacare.

RMD must happen starting at age 72 on these accounts or there is a 50 % penalty on the money that is not withdrawn. Why is this a significant problem? Because no one is telling you to "plan" before 72 and by the time you get to 72, you have lost 10-20 years of planning to reduce your overall tax liability on your major retirement accounts.

What's the Point?

Most experts agree that tax rates must go up in the future. Most experts are also now saying that you may not be in a lower tax bracket when you retire. By the time you are going to retire, you have paid off your house, you lost college tax credits, and kids are gone so you have lost all these deductions.

Lower your tax liability on your retirement accounts that will require a required minimum distribution no later than 72 years of age...

Contribute into Roth 401ks, Roth IRA'S, Roth 403/TSA's

Convert IRA's and 401K's in a systematic strategic plan

I want to give you the best advice no one is giving right now....

Rey Cruz, CFP® is an author, financial educator, Estate and Wealth planning specialist, and planned giving consultant to leading charities.

One of the region's top wealth and retirement planning specialists, Cruz has been heard on many radio stations throughout Chicago. Rey is currently the financial guru on 95.9 "The River" radio station. As the creator of "Cruzing into Retirement™" system, Rey has been helping individuals and families prepare for and enjoy their ideal retirement since 1985 and is a member of Ed Slott's Master Elite IRA Advisor Group™.

Rey Cruz has been an active leader in Aurora community; having served on more that 10 non-for-profit boards. As much as Rey enjoys serving in the community, he also has a love of baseball. He has sponsored teams in the North Aurora Baseball Association and coached his daughter's softball team as a batting coach.

CHAD DISBENNETT

Run with Those Running Faster Than You!

"We all have dreams. But in order to make dreams come into reality, it takes an awful lot of determination, dedication, self-discipline, and effort."
—Jesse Owens, legendary American track star

············ TIPS ···············

1. It starts with the proper mindset and attitude
2. Build a Dream Team—Invest in other people's talent
3. Create a Tax Free Retirement Strategy

·································

Taxes: A Minefield or A Goldmine?

"If you are born poor it's not your mistake, but if you die poor it's your mistake."
—Bill Gates

"Taxes are killing us, Chad..."

That's how my conversation began with Brian Johnson (not their real name for privacy purposes), a well-known and very successful business owner, who attended one of our recent Private Briefings and signed up for the Wealth With Clarity 2nd Opinion.

When Brian came in, he said, "Last week, when you said, 'The IRS tax code is either a minefield or a goldmine' at your Private Briefing, I almost jumped out of my chair. I couldn't get that out of my mind. That's why we have been so excited to get time with you to find out what that means for us. I got to tell you. We don't mind paying our share, but when you showed us that the top 10 percent of income earners are shouldering 70 percent of the tax burden, well, frankly, that makes me pretty mad. We started with nothing and I appreciate the opportunities we have been given; but we have worked hard, very hard and we have sacrificed to save our money."

"I get it," I said to them. "I believe that you deserve to keep more of what you earn. That's our mission. To help business owners, healthcare professionals and independent woman preserve, protect and pass on their hard-earned wealth. Taxes are just one of the wealth predators."

According to the Tax Foundation, in 1955, the Internal Revenue Code had less than a half a million words. Since then, it has mushroomed almost five times that to 2.4 million words. The tax code isn't the only thing that Americans must deal with to complete their taxes. There are another 7.7 million words of tax regulations from the IRS and around 60,000 pages of case law that is tax related. That's over 72,000 pages that is a minefield if you don't know how to use it to your benefit. Or, a goldmine if you are trained to know where and how to use the opportunities.

"However, it takes a commitment to fully take advantage of the tax and financial opportunities," I told them. "The most important component of commitment is mindset. It takes three mindsets to live an abundant lifestyle and leave a lasting legacy."

"What are the mindsets?" Brian asked.

Mindset #1: Strategic Delegation

If you have accumulated over $1,000,000 (one million dollars), you are in a very unique category. Only 3 percent of Americans have built wealth in excess of $1,000,000.

The strongest wealth builders have realized this simple fact: they focus on what they are really good at and delegate the rest. They don't focus on strengthening their weaknesses, but instead find people whose strengths complement their weaknesses and they hire them. Most wealth builders understand that they grew their wealth focusing on their strengths and hiring the rest. This is what we call a "strategic delegation."

I used to love to help my father work on the old brown Ford truck we had when I was growing up. Standing right beside my dad with one foot on a stool and the other on the front bumper while leaning over the engine, I learned the basics of how to change the oil and replace the spark plugs.

Have you looked under the hood of the cars today? It's like looking under the hood of a space ship. My brother-in-law is an expert mechanic that spends nearly 10 hours a day, six days a week working on automobiles. If I have a problem, I hire him.

Building wealth is a complex task requiring a full-time team of specialists. The most important areas of life require specialists: health, wealth, and pilots.

Mindset #2: Open Minded

Successful wealth builders are open minded. They are open to new ideas, because they know that there is no monopoly on new ideas. Legendary basketball coach, John Wooden, winner of nine National Championships, said, "It's what we learn after we know it all that makes all the difference in the world."

Think of it this way. Imagine a box that represents the universe of understanding of you and your present advisors. If there are strategies, concepts and ideas outside of your present box that can reduce your taxes, enhance your income and allow you to leave more to your family and charity, are you open to them?

"The measure of intelligence is the ability to change. The mind that opens to a new idea never returns to its original size." Albert Einstein

When Dr. Fred Simon (not his real name), a family practitioner, saw that he could decrease his income taxes and enhance his lifestyle with less risk, his natural reaction was, "How come I didn't know this?"

"You're not supposed to," I said. "If I came to you for a second opinion and you showed me that my health could be improved, I wouldn't wonder why I didn't know. That's your job."

"How come my present advisors didn't tell me... and what will they say?" Fred asked.

I said, "There are only three things your present advisors can say. First, they could say, 'I didn't know.'"

"That would be professional suicide," Fred said.

"They could say, 'I knew and didn't tell you.'" I said.

"Then I'd kill them," Fred shot back.

When a second opinion opens new opportunities, present advisors can only say something like, "Oh, sure I knew, but you shouldn't do anything differently."

If what you were doing with your wealth isn't going to get you where you want to go; or if there are unknown side effects under your current plan; or if there are tax reduction or income enhancing opportunities you are missing, how soon would you like to know?

"We all need people who will give us feedback. That's how we improve," says Bill Gates, one of the richest people in the world.

Mindset #3: Take Action

Jim Rohn, business owner, author and teacher, reportedly worth around $500 million, said, "Don't let your learning lead to knowledge, or you become a fool. Let your learning lead to action, and you can become wealthy."

Michelle Duncan (not her real name either), a recently divorced ER nurse, came to see me after one of our Private Briefings. She had worked with a lot of different advisers over the years, but she had never worked with a specialist to build an integrated financial and lifestyle plan. After the divorce, she said, she was very concerned about protecting her money, making sure she had enough income and leaving something to her two girls.

"I'm kind of a do-it-yourselfer. I like to stay in control," Michelle said.

"If you were building your dream house, would you act as the architect to create the blueprint; the general contractor to hire the subs and manage the building; and the subs to build the house," I asked.

The recent DIY craze has created the false (and dangerous) myth that you can architect, build and maintain your own financial future.

"Control the process, but you can't go it alone. I created The Wealth With Clarity Process so successful professionals like you can stay in total control, while we help you blueprint your ideal future, uncover the unknown side effects under your current plan and build a wealth engine that gives you security and peace of mind." I said.

After going through The Wealth With Clarity Process, we uncovered 7 dangers, inconsistencies and gaps under her current plan, that she was not even aware of.

"This is frustrating in one sense. I thought everything was good. I try to keep up and I get input from a number of advisors," she said.

"What would you tell me if I showed up in the ER and said I was my own doctor," I asked. "Michelle, what if there were ways to position your hard-earned dollars so that you would never have to pay ANY taxes on them in the future? What if you could also arrange it so that you would never be hurt by a market crash or downturn in the future, and even better you would be able to capitalize each and every time the pundits on Capitol Hill and Wall Street screwed up our economy?"

"Chad, please create and build a wealth plan that keeps me and my money safe," added Michelle.

A comprehensive approach to her money and future gave her more options to choose from to decrease her taxes and increase her income for an upgraded lifestyle. The extra wealth created will allow her to pass on a nice legacy to her girls, and to the hospital. It also gave her more control of her money and her future.

As Seneca said long ago, "Wealth is the slave of a wise man. The master of a fool."

Strategic Delegation. Open Minded. Action.

We always stress with our clients the importance of making the commitment and having the three mindsets. We then look to discover options to save taxes and increase their retirement income, while better protecting their hard-earned money.

Are you taking advantage of every tax reducing, income increasing, lifestyle enhancing option you can?

It's not what you make, it's what you keep!

That's why we created the Wealth With Clarity 2nd Opinion, so you can be absolutely sure you are doing everything you can, and not missing any option, to keep your hard-earned money safe and working for you.

It's a confidential opportunity to discover tax saving and income enhancing options, you may not even be aware are available to you. Our mission is to help successful Business Owners, Healthcare Professionals and independent Women take advantage of all the available options to upgrade their lifestyle and preserve, protect and pass on their wealth.

To get more information and resources to help you grow your wealth, you can go to our website WealthWithClarity.com and request any of our special reports.

Are taxes a minefield or a goldmine for you? It's up to you!

Chad Disbennett, CFP® is a nationally recognized **Financial Educator, Author, Speaker and Retirement Planner.** As founder and CEO, Chad and his team at Disbennett Wealth Management Group have been helping Business Owners, Health Care Professionals, and Women on their own, learn how to preserve, protect, and pass on their wealth.

With a background in education, Chad created the Wealth With Clarity™ Process to help his clients better understand the sometimes-confusing world of Financial Planning. He is a true financial "Coach" in that he thoroughly enjoys learning about his clients and their needs, and then finding the best solutions to fit those needs. As opposed to simply being an advisor, he is a true guide to his clients, and believes in custom solutions.

Chad graduated from the College of Business at the University of Cincinnati, and then continued his education at Capital University in the realm of business education. He holds several securities and insurance designations and completed the rigorous training necessary to become a Certified Financial Planner™ Practitioner through The Ohio State University.

To learn more about Chad, and for additional tips on Retirement Planning, you can visit ChadDisbennett.com or WealthWithClairty.com. There you will find upcoming events, useful tools and reports that are available to download.

PETER DOBRICH

Success to Significance: When you're gone, what do you *really* want to leave behind?

> "Not everything that is faced can be changed. But nothing can be changed until it is faced."
> —James Baldwin

············ **TIPS** ················

1. Face the issues—behavioural change
2. Equalization—game plan
3. Generational Wealth—your Life print

································

Jane and Alice had meant to get lunch together for some time. It had been six months since the funeral; time has a way of sneaking up on you.

Alice's husband, Henry, had built a successful tool-and-die enterprise from the ground up. He was nearly ready to pass along his seat at the head of the boardroom table to his eldest son when he dropped dead on the golf course, a few steps before the turn. The doctors said it was a stroke. He would have been 65 that month.

Half a year later, Jane expected to find Alice in improving spirits—still grieving, of course, but comfortable in the knowledge that she and her husband had built a formidable foundation for their family over their three decades together.

Today, however, Alice's mind seemed to be elsewhere.

"I've always said that everything has its way of working itself out," she said somberly, nervously tracing the circumference of her soup bowl with her spoon. "We just thought everything was okay, kind of like everybody else does."

As Jane learned, Alice's eldest son was now running the company, but his sister, who'd moved overseas years earlier, was now agitating for her share in the family fortune. What's more, a former business partner of Henry's was challenging the estate. Alice hadn't heard his name in what felt like decades.

Alice had never considered herself a political person; the government was always there in the background, like a dull ache that flared up in the wrist when it was going to rain, but she lived her day-to-day life without worrying much about what goes on in the corridors of power.

Following Henry's death, though, she found herself faced with a staggering tax bill and quickly got to grips with once-foreign terms like "in probate" and "liquidate."

The long, painful process of selling off assets—including the family's vacation homes and vehicles—soon began in earnest. After the first sale, she wasn't able to get anywhere near market value for anything else. Word had gotten out, and the vultures were at the gate.

It was already autumn and she still hadn't booked this year's trip to Naples.

Everything Alice and husband had worked so hard to build—and everything she had sacrificed to allow this to happen—seemed to be under threat. What would her income be at this time next year? What was it now?

An ill-conceived and poorly executed will, it turns out, is a disaster. Alice and Henry hadn't received the right advice.

Jane hadn't noticed earlier, but their table felt like the centre of attention. She could feel several pairs of eyes fixed on their conversation from across the club. Did they all know already?

Before Henry's death, Jane and Alice's husbands had been close. They were friendly business rivals, but their work was different enough to keep them out of direct competition—and what is it they say about a rising tide lifting all boats?

In many ways, the two women had lived parallel lives up until then. Jane's eldest daughter was well on her way to taking over their family business, but her other children wanted little to do with it. One son was waiting on a medical school acceptance letter, the other—somewhat more optimistically—a big festival slot for his fledgling band. Both would need significant financial help, in their own way, in the coming years.

After lunch, Jane walked back to her car feeling tired. She had some heavy questions for her own husband later that night.

***

Tragically, Alice's family didn't have a viable financial plan in place.

Stories like this one are all too common in my professional world. Time and time again, disaster strikes, and a family finds itself torn apart by the poor succession planning of the very business built to benefit and sustain it.

It doesn't have to be this way.

My clients may want initially to discuss their investment returns, but I don't see that as where my value proposition resides. I can put a bakery full of pie graphs on the wall, but what I really want to do is ask a simple question: What's on your mind? I need to know what you and your family really *want* to happen. Then, it's my job to work with you to establish a long-term strategic plan to get you there—and to protect you and yours from Alice's fate.

What we do is create *certainty*—guaranteed liquidity at the most difficult point for a businessperson. If cash is king, stable income-generating assets are practically deities. Long-term financial planning is about knitting together a safety net, as stocks, properties, and other assets that need to be liquidated might not be there to catch you when you fall. Imagine we have another 2008, your assets are suddenly worth 40 percent less than they were a year ago, and you or your children need money right away.

Here are a few things I've learned during my career in wealth management:

Behavioural Change: Facing the Issues Head On

Personalities are the most important currency in the business world. Typically, successful entrepreneurs are charismatic, strong-willed, opinionated people. You probably know a few!

The thing is, the same alpha-dog traits that drive business excellence can set your family up for future failure.

I get it! You are where you are because you've solved every problem to this point through your own ingenuity and sheer force of will. You haven't needed anybody else's help, so why start now?

For this reason, many find legacy planning frustrating, but I like to persuade my clients to look at laying long-term plans as a *reward* rather than an obligation of success. When you buy a new house or car, the gratification is immediate, but I'm in a quieter, more slowly rewarding line of work. At first, the reward is invisible, but what we do in our industry is something valuable that only the relatively prosperous can access.

The truth is, most people fail to deal with their greatest challenges head on. They attempt to outrun them or meet them meekly from the side. There is an expression I've grown fond of over the years: "The nail you're sitting on may not hurt anymore, but it's the rust that's going to kill you." When we don't deal with our problems, we can find ways to live painlessly in the moment, but the long-term infection only grows stronger.

Often, it takes a painful experience—or the threat of one—to kick-start a serious change of behaviour. Great things rarely start to happen from within the restrictive box of one's comfort zone.

As the saying goes, smart people learn from their own mistakes; wise people learn from other people's. Think of your financial advisor as an encyclopedia of your neighbours, peers, and competitors' mistakes. Look: we've seen and been through it all. Chances are, we already understand your situation; usually, it's easier to solve than you might think!

One's relationship with a wealth management professional should always be more than merely transactional, but it is still that. At the end of the day, my clients employ me to perform a service: to work collectively, along with their boards of directors and other most trusted advisors, to *get it done*. But it's up to you to make the first call.

Equalization: What's Your Game Plan?

Imagine a successful business owner has three children. One of them, the daughter, is poised to take over the enterprise. She grew up in the business and is made for the work. That's great, but what about her two brothers, neither of whom works with her? How do they get their fair share?

Equalization doesn't necessarily mean dividing and distributing one's assets as neat, equal portions. It's about making sure everybody's taken care of *fairly*—whatever that means for their circumstances. Naturally, the more children you have, the more complicated it can get.

You don't want to leave the equalization decision in the hands of that one sibling who will ultimately inherit the operation. Resentment is a very poisonous feeling, and so is envy.

The best course of action is to get the right parties in the room across from the right intermediary—somebody who can moderate the parents' decisions and articulate the reasons for them. Assuming we've built a strong enough relationship with someone, that's usually our role. If I'm not the right person, *find* the right person. (Hint: It's probably not your lawyer.)

In an estate plan, it's important to consider capital gains tax on a business, the short-term liquidity needs of that business, and an emergency succession plan were something to happen to the founder.

Equalization can take the form of a series of significant lump-sum payments upon a parent's death, or it can be parceled out annually over a person's lifetime.

Usually, a sound equalization plan involves putting a solid liquidity strategy for the business in place according to its value. Ideally, with sufficient planning, there is no need to assume unnecessary risk by relying on banks for capital. Consider a scenario in which you *haven't* established a liquidity plan and need to approach a bank for money. Does the bank have a relationship with the new leader of the business? Does it like and trust her enough to loan enough capital to make sure her brothers get paid out?

Here, the daughter *wants* to take up the reins, but this is not always the case. Often, a child will submit to a strong parent's will out of an innate sense of duty, or a profound but misplaced desire to make them proud. Often, business leader casts a long shadow, which can inhibit their children from growing bright personalities of their own. If you run a business, have you introduced your child to the important relationships that keep it running? Those will need to become *their* relationships as well, if they aren't already, if the business is going to outlive you. Consider that 70% of first-generation businesses fail, but fully 90% of second-generation businesses fail.

In many cases, neither parent nor child will allow themselves to stop and ask a critical question: Is the child actually *interested* in the business?

I see it all the time: The child doesn't share their parent's passion but doesn't know how to tell them. They go to the office every day, they don't like it, the misery follows them home, and it ends up being radioactive.

It can be uncomfortable, but somebody has to bring this discussion to the table.

In many cases, the wisest course of action is to go to the capital markets, get the maximum value for the business, and distribute that new wealth equitably across the family.

Generational Wealth: What's Your Life Print?

Nobody wants to foreground their own mortality, but we're in the business of "it could all end tomorrow"; life can change in the time it takes to shuffle a stack of tax returns, so why not reconceptualize the conversation? Let's talk about the people and passions you love the most in the world, and how they're going to live wealthily. What a meaningful, powerful discussion to have!

Ultimately, the journey that happens in my office leads someone from *success* to *significance*.

If you're reading this book, chances are you're somebody people talk about. What are the odds those conversations stop after you're gone? Imagine finding out the most successful, streetwise businessperson left their empire to crumble to dust because they never got around to putting an appropriate succession plan in place. What kind of legacy is that?

Think about your legacy as a *life print*—the indelible impression you make on the world, and an enduring record of your contribution to your community during your time on earth.

Like a thumbprint, a life print is unique and detailed. No two are identical, and some of the intricate, curving lines they comprise are more prominent and easier to trace than others.

One's family is almost always part of their life print, but that only makes up part of the picture. Perhaps your ideal legacy involves a major donation or sustaining an annual annuity payment to the sleepaway camp where you spent every summer as a child. Possibly your perfect picture includes your parish, or maybe your alma mater. Whatever you envision, there are ways to make that happen.

Here's another way of looking at it: Think of your business as a fruit tree that you planted early in your life. We want to make sure your family picks from it indefinitely, because its roots are so deep, they weather all storms. In other words, what will today's decision mean when your great grandchild is born?

Over the years, there will be pressure at times to uproot and transplant that tree, but this is rarely the best course of action. By the third move, the plant will have suffered. Sometimes, even the heartiest tree might not get fruit in a year. But it will again. Be patient.

Many people view legacy planning as a means to set up cushy, insulated lives for their children—more comfortable that their own, and without the work! In reality, safeguarding generational wealth is about making sure our kids are protected against all eventualities. Really, putting responsible, productive plans in place for your children it's a natural extension of the entire project of parenting. It's about looking out for your own.

For example, in Canada, the popular understanding is that we enjoy uncomplicated universal access to some of the world's best healthcare. But what if we didn't?

This is a conversation I have with my clients all the time: Considering the direction we're heading, with our rapidly aging population, I can't imagine the Canadian healthcare system as we currently know it is sustainable. Now, more than ever, families need even more wealth than they might think: If life-sustaining medical care becomes more expensive or difficult to access in the future, your children will need to have a formidable healthcare fund in place.

Moreover, I don't want my children under the finger of the government. Imagine a future in which industrious Canadians labour under a 60-percent marginal tax rate, creating a situation where it's almost impossible to get ahead. As the government continues to find ways to increase its revenue on our backs, I want my clients' family wealth to be able to fill in the gaps created, to enable the next generation to live the lives they want while still enjoying a sense of financial security.

If that sounds like something you want, too, isn't it time we talked? Provided you're prepared to face your issues head on and change your behaviour when needed, as establishing a solid equalization game plan and deepening your life print are much more realistic than you might think.

Peter Dobrich is the founder of the boutique advisory firm Private Financial Group. For 25 years, he has expertly guided high-net-worth families and entrepreneurs by helping them navigate their most critical financial decisions.

Peter was part-owner of the Ontario Hockey League's Windsor Spitfires for seven years. Under his stewardship, the team revitalized its flagging brand, won two national championships, and negotiated the construction of a state-of-the-art mixed-use facility that constitutes a remarkable community legacy.

Business is in Peter's DNA: He learned the real value of a dollar growing up in his family's food-service operation, which grew from humble beginnings to support more than 60 families for over three decades.

Similarly, Peter built PFG from the ground up, having already launched a successful flooring treatment business while studying finance at the University of Windsor.

Peter believes nothing important can be solved without a deep discussion. Isn't it time you talked?

NAVI DOWTY

The Worst Retirement Income Strategy That Almost Everyone is Using

"A fine is a tax for doing something wrong. A tax is a fine for doing something right."
—Anonymous

• • • • • • • • • • • • • • • TIPS • • • • • • • • • • • • • • •

1. Test whether you should pull your retirement money first or last-if you get this wrong it could be worth millions of dollars
2. Save Taxes—Your tax return is either filled with land mines or filled with gold mines
3. Buy the Best—Don't lose money

Ben Wise, (not his real name), a well-known business owner in my area, came to one of my classes. He came up to me afterward and said, "I had no idea about any of these nine myths.

This was not only eye-opening, but I'd like to come in to see you. You and I need to talk as soon as possible. I had no idea that these myths were leading to some costly mistakes. I'm so glad that I came to your class today."

I hear that repeatedly. People are often worried about their retirement savings. They will say, "I've been rich, and I've been poor, and I never want to be poor again."

Imagine being able to enjoy retirement without having to open the newspaper, turn on the financial TV shows, or look at your phone every hour to monitor your investments.

The only way that's possible is if you uncover the mistakes that nobody is talking about because the mistakes are based on myths that you may believe are true. Here I'm going to outline 3 of them. The rest are outlined in a special report that I make available to people who reach out to me.

Myth Number One
You should pour as much money into your retirement accounts as possible.

Overfunding your retirement accounts is a mistake.

Fred Unfortunate, (not his real name of course), came to one of my retirement planning and tax savings classes.

He is a retired executive with a leading company who had planned on a comfortable retirement with his wife and three children. He retired in February 2000 with just over $2,000,000. Fifteen years after he retired, he had about 6% of his original retirement accounts left, and he was living largely on Social Security. This breaks my heart. He had believed in these myths and had not considered the rising costs, market fluctuations, and taxes. He had no pension or any guaranteed income other than his Social Security.

Fred waited far too long to learn how to avoid these mistakes. It's kind of like going to the doctor and saying that you want to get healthy, and they find out that your arteries are 98% blocked.

There's not a whole lot that they can do at that point.

If you are like most of the people I meet with, you probably have way too much money in your tax-deferred accounts. These would be accounts like your IRA's, 401k's and 403b's. They all have slightly different rules, but they have these things in common.

You get a deduction when you put money into these accounts, and they are taxed as ordinary income when you take the money out.

You are required to take money out starting at age 70 1/2 or you get a big penalty. Congress will probably push this age up to 72 or later in the future. But there will always be some age at which you have to start paying the taxes that you deferred. You also get penalized if you take money out too early. And you are limited as to how much you can put into these accounts.

So, if you take money out too early, too late or put in too much, you are penalized. You have been told all your life that it is a good idea to pour as much as possible into these tax-deferred retirement accounts. Up until recently, it made sense to defer your taxes because tax rates have been declining since the end of the second world war.

But as I point out in Myth number two, taxes are going up. When?

January 1, 2026 taxes go up about 25% at a minimum for most taxpayers.

Here is another reason that you may not want to put too much money into your retirement accounts.

The best-taxed assets that you can invest in are capital gain assets. These would be things like stocks or Real Estate. Most of the return on these types of assets are on the gains, not the income. When you sell these assets, you get preferential tax treatment. But if you put stocks or real estate into your retirement accounts, you magically transform them from the best-taxed assets into the worst-taxed assets. The IRS has a special term for withdrawals that you take out of retirement accounts. They call it ordinary income. That means that withdrawals from your retirement accounts are taxed just like your wages or the interest that you earn.

Even if tax rates didn't go up, there are other reasons that you may not want to overfund your tax-deferred retirement accounts today. When you take taxable money out in the future, the very act of adding that income to your tax bottom line may push you into a higher tax bracket. It most likely will also cause tax on your Social Security. Also, when your heirs inherit your retirement accounts, they will have to pay the tax at their perhaps higher tax brackets.

And of course, the brackets themselves are likely to be higher for you in the future.

Of course, if your employer is matching the contributions to your retirement accounts, take the free money.

But beware of overfunding these accounts. If you do, you will create a tax problem that you may not be able to solve. If you have too much money in your tax-deferred retirement accounts, you will be facing tax Armageddon when the rates go back up.

Of course, there is always the other major problem of overfunding your retirement accounts.

Almost all the money in retirement accounts is in the stock market. Buying stocks, mutual funds, and ETF's thru dollar cost averaging every month thru contributions to your retirement accounts is a fantastic accumulation strategy. It is not such a good preservation and distribution strategy.

As you near retirement, you probably don't want to experience a repeat of 2000 or 2008 when most people saw their retirement accounts cut in half or worse. There will be another 2008. And this time, you may be withdrawing money to live on in retirement, causing the inevitable downturns to cause your retirement accounts to spiral down even faster. I call it dollar cost averaging in reverse. If your account goes down 50% you must make 100% to get back to even!

It is much worse if you are withdrawing money to live on or for required minimum distributions.

Act today! Reach out to me now so you can find out about other options for you.

Myth Number Two
Taxes are Going Down

Staking your retirement plans on the hope that taxes are going to go down is a major mistake!

The problem is that taxes are going up.

When you ask? At the latest, taxes are going to go up on January 1, 2026, when the new tax law expires, and everything reverts to the 2017 rules. For most people in America, this will be a 25% increase. For instance, going from the 12% to the 15% tax bracket.

David Walker, the former controller general of the US Government, told Congress that taxes must double. He probably knows more about the finances of the federal government than anyone on the planet. If he is right about taxes doubling, that will put taxes back to about what they were in the early sixties.

That is much lower than the 94% top rate in the last two years of the second world war, but it will be a major financial shock for the 78 million baby boomers retiring.

Remember that the top 10% of taxpayers pay nearly 70% of the taxes collected by the Federal Government! If you are reading this book, that is most likely you. The truth is that our income tax rates have been coming down for all our lives.

Federal Income taxes are low right now in historical terms. However, our total tax burden continues to rise. In 2019, April 29th was Tax Freedom Day. You spent the first one-third of the year working to pay all the different levels of government their cut of your hard work.

Since we live in the greatest country in the history of the world, paying for all these taxes doesn't seem out of reason.

However, as Arthur Godfrey used to say, "I'm proud to be able to pay taxes in America. But I could be just as proud for half the taxes." With nearly 74,000 pages of the tax code, regulations, rulings, and court cases, there is plenty of room for problems to occur.

Many financial advisors that you encounter will tell you that the tax code is littered with tax traps. I think it is littered with opportunities. I say, let's go searching for gold on your tax return. After all, about one-third of the code deals with the taxation of income. The other two-thirds is about the deductions.

There are endless interactions between different tax code sections. For instance, when retiring you will find that your Social Security is probably going to be taxed because of how you have your finances arranged. "What?" You say. "It felt like a tax when I paid it, and now I have to pay a tax when I start receiving it?" Yes, you do if your retirement accounts are arranged in a way to cause this taxation on your Social Security. Unfortunately, almost all are arranged that way. Most people reading this will be paying tax on 85% of their Social Security.

That tax payment causes a hole in your retirement income. Where does the money come from to fill that hole? More withdrawals from your retirement accounts, of course, causing those accounts to spiral down even faster.

Myth Number Three
Inflation is Dead

Staking your retirement hopes on the mistaken belief that inflation is a thing of the past is a big mistake.

Your costs to live are going up. Studies show that your medical costs and housing costs are rising faster than the general rate of inflation. This is one of the reasons that the CPI-E, the inflation index for people over 62 is about 7% higher than the CPI-U, the index for all urban consumers. The big components of the cost of living index are housing, medical care, food, and transportation.

One in three people is going to need additional care in retirement. You must decide whether you want Motel 3 care or luxury care.

Even Motel 3 care is going cost six or seven thousand dollars per month, and that is if you don't live near a major city or need more than just custodial care. If you have medical issues or need memory care, the cost is much higher. And it is rising fast.

A recent study found that the average couple is likely to spend over $285,000 for medical care in retirement.

Look at your recent property tax bills. Are they going up? That is a part of the housing component of the index. Almost all the towns and cities are starving for tax revenue.

I can tell you this. I used to develop income-producing real estate. In the residential sector, property taxes were about 15% of the gross rent. Property taxes are now nearly 30% of the rent, and there seems to be no end in sight for the increases. The local governments share of the rent has nearly doubled!

Have you replaced a roof lately? How about siding, gutters, or windows? These costs have gone up in most parts of the country.

Just look at anything that you buy online and compare last year's costs with a recent purchase. You will probably see at least a 10% increase.

For the affluent, these cost increases are not a very big deal, but they are indicative of the general increase in costs.

People tell me all the time that they put 2% or 3% cost increases into their calculation of how much their living costs would rise in retirement. I think that is low. I hope that it is only 4%, but I don't think that is reasonable.

Even at 4%, your costs to live will double every 18 years. We seem to be in an era of rising interest rates. Rates bottomed out in 2017 at only 2.2% for the 30-year treasury bond. Would you lend money out for 30 years at only 2.2%? Of course not.

I believe 2.2% is the low point any of us will see in our lifetime. What has that got to do with inflation? Interest rates and inflation go hand in hand. An investor will always want to get more interest for lending out their money than the rate of inflation. Otherwise, they are sliding backward.

I don't know if inflation will ever get back to where it was in 1982 when it was 18%. I hope not. At 18%, your costs double every four years! Think of that. Hopefully, we will not see that time again. But even at only 4%, which is low in my estimation, your costs are likely to double at least twice during your retirement or second career years. And that is if no major medical or unexpected financial emergencies arise.

The issues that you face today are likely the same issues that you faced three years ago.

Most likely they'll be the same issues you face three years from now unless you act.

Act today.

We have developed our popular Retirement Opportunity Conversation.

It is a complimentary, no-obligation, 57-minute conversation in which you can share your details confidentially. You can get your questions answered without pressure to do anything.

You have three assurances:

1. There is nothing to buy. It is my way of adding value first.
2. You will discover some new opportunities that exist for you and your family. And you will uncover some obstacles that stand in the way of your ideal retirement.
3. You will leave knowing what to do next if anything.

This is part of our core values, which is to give value first.

To get the rest of the myths or to schedule your complimentary Retirement Opportunity Conversation, call 630-893-4142, 715-845-4367, or email a request to Navi@NaviDowty.com

As the founder of Navi Dowty & Associates, Inc. and a CHARTERED FINANCIAL ANALYST™, a designation held by less than 1% of the financial advisor community, Navi embraces the idea of getting the most streams of tax advantaged income as possible for each client. He recognizes that for most people, taxes are their biggest expense.

Since the early 1970's, Navi Dowty has seen many economic cycles and is passing on what he has learned to others.

He started investing with money he earned delivering papers and bailing hay in middle school.

He began investing in, developing and managing investment real estate in the early 70's and expanded into the estate planning and securities markets in the early 80's when interest rates had skyrocketed. He noticed that his real estate clients were mostly interested in the tax savings and so he has focused his planning for his affluent clients around the idea of saving taxes, since the mid 80's.

You may have seen him speaking at Harvard, Nasdaq, West Point, and on numerous TV shows. He has acted as a professional continuing education educator, an expert witness and a nationally recognized tax and income planner.

He is the creator of the unique, proprietary, trademarked, Smiling Retiree Process™

JOHN P. DUBOTS

We Don't Know What We Don't Know

"Success is peace of mind which is a direct result of self-satisfaction in knowing you made the effort to become the best of which you are capable."
—John Wooden, Head Coach

• • • • • • • • • • • • • • • **TIPS** • • • • • • • • • • • • • • •

1. The importance of avoiding losses.
2. Don't overlook Taxes and the cost of Healthcare in Retirement.
3. Guaranteed Sources of Income in Retirement are key.

• •

Although there are several other concerns, I have heard from those in retirement or about to retire these are without question the most common. So, before we talk about how to overcome these concerns or obstacles let me tell you how I got to where I am today.

I started in the financial services industry in 1991 right out of graduate school. I had just graduated from the University of New Hampshire with a Master of Public Administration and had completed my undergraduate degree, a B.S. in Resource Economics. I was fortunate to go to school on a football scholarship and really enjoyed my time in New England. When I graduated at the end of 1990 the economy in New England was in a recession and I grew up in a small town in north central Pennsylvania that offered very little career opportunity. I had worked throughout college for a large cable television company during the summers, and did an internship for the city of Portsmouth, New Hampshire as part of my master's degree. While I was there, I created a plan for the redevelopment of Pease Air Force Base. I learned two things from my experiences. One, I didn't want to have to climb the corporate ladder and sit behind someone for years before I would get my opportunity to be a manager. Two, I knew I didn't want to work in the public sector where it seemed impossible to be able to make people happy while having to work with a tight budget. So, in February of 1991 I set off from Coudersport, PA to California having never been there before. I landed in Palm Springs with a friend who was there doing an internship and found a job at a local night club as a "bouncer". This provided me the opportunity to interview during the day and find my career. I employed the services of an employment company which set up some interviews for me, but the jobs really weren't what I wanted so, I began to search the newspapers myself. I found an ad that caught my attention. It touted "management and income potential". This seemed to be exactly what I was looking for. I went for an interview, was invited back for a second interview and was offered the job. This was the beginning of my career in financial services.

When I started my career in financial services, I didn't know the first thing about it, but went through what I thought at the time was a thorough and rigorous training program. I obtained my Series 6, 63, 24, 26 and life insurance license and eventually my Series 7 and 65. I spent my time selling "packaged products" to clients offering them mutual funds, variable annuities and life insurance. I moved through the ranks fairly quickly and was soon promoted to District Manager. At the time I was to be promoted to Branch Manager, I realized I was building a business for someone else and had learned the business to know at this point I could go out on my own and have my own business, so in June of 1994 I left the company and started Dubots Capital Management. I continued to work with young married couples helping them to save for retirement and it wouldn't be until 2002 that I would come to the realization the financial services industry was broken. It is broken as far as helping consumers and it is broken with regard to how financial advisors work with clients. Let me explain. When I got into the financial services industry I was taught (and what all financial advisors are taught) is to "buy and hold, invest for the long term. We know the market fluctuates but moves in an upward trend over the long term". All of which is true by the way. Today I call this riding the roller coaster of the stock market. So that if you have enough time to ride out the ups and downs of the stock market you will be okay. But for most people they don't have the stomach to do this. Ask yourself this question, "who's best interest is it for you to always be fully invested, yours or the financial services company?" When you understand the answer to that question you will understand why financial companies and their representatives teach buy and hold. Here's what happened that changed my career.

In 2000 the S&P 500 was down 10%, in 2001 it was down another 13% and in 2002 in lost another 23%. The first year you were fine with my explanation that the market was down 10% and you were down 10%. "Hang in there, we know the market fluctuates, but it will come back." The next year you were down another 13% and after 2002 you were tired of hearing me say, "Hang in there we know the stock market fluctuates but moves in an upward trend".

I called a client near the end of 2002 to schedule an account review with them and they said to me, "John, I don't need you to lose my money for me, I can do that well enough on my own." In that instant I realized he was right, and it wasn't just him, it was all my clients, it was my family and myself that had just lost nearly fifty percent of their retirement savings over the last three years. I realized there had to be a better way than to tell people to hang in there and everything would be okay. So, I went outside my firm to research and do due diligence to find investment strategies that would help protect my clients. What I found were two strategies we use today to help our clients protect their portfolios in times of market downturns. The first is risk managed portfolios and the second is indexing strategies. Now, within this chapter I won't try to explain these two strategies, but I will talk to you about three important tips in planning for a successful retirement.

Understanding the importance of avoiding losses. Traditional financial planning teaches us that the younger we are the more risk we can take because time is on your side. I would argue that whether you are thirty years old or sixty-five you would be better off having not lost 30%. The first thing I teach my clients is the Math of Gains and Losses. What most people don't understand is that when you lose 20% it's not 20% that gets you back to breakeven. You would need to earn 25% just to breakeven. However, if I told you that you lost 20% this year and made 20% the next, most people would think, "Okay, I didn't make any money, but I also didn't lose any money" and that's not true. You would have would have lost 4%. If I had told you that you lost 20% this year and made 25% the next most people would think they have money, but in fact you would have just broken even, and your return would be zero. If you lose 40% you need 66.7% to get back to even and a 50% loss requires a 100% gain to get you back to where you were. Unfortunately, this happened to many retirees and pre-retirees in the stock market correction of 2008 -2009. So, understanding this concept of avoiding losses is extremely important particularly when you are entering into retirement and will begin taking income from your portfolio. This leads to understanding the sequence of returns and how during the accumulation phase of your life, the order in which you receive returns has no impact on the outcome of your portfolio. However, when you begin to take distributions it has a significant outcome on your retirement nest egg and whether you will have enough money to last throughout your lifetime.

Don't' Overlook Taxes and the cost of Healthcare in Retirement. We've all heard the saying, "It's not what you make, but what you keep that counts". Well it's no different in retirement. You must account for taxes in your income plan when planning for retirement. Now most of us have been told that when you retire you will be in a lower tax bracket and that may be true. But this is another falsehood that traditional financial planning teaches us. The truth is that most people find they are in the same or higher tax bracket when they retire. Most retirees that I have worked with want to maintain their standard of living and their income in retirement. Regarding today's tax rates we are in a relatively low tax rate environment with the top marginal tax bracket being 37%. In the 1970's the top marginal tax bracket was 70% and shortly after World War II the top marginal bracket was 90%! The reason I bring this up is because as I write this our country's current national debt exceeds TWENTY-TWO TRILLION dollars!!! With an unfunded deficit including social security and Medicare of over ONE HUNDRED TWENTY TRILLION dollars!!! At some point this bill will need to be paid and I have a secret for you, it will be the taxpayers that pay the bill. That's right, you and me. There are only two, maybe three ways to fix this problem. One, reduce benefits. Two, increase taxes or some combination of the two. The Social Security trust fund released their annual report for 2018 and reported the trust fund would be depleted in the year 2035. This doesn't mean you will no longer receive a social security check, but it does mean your benefit will be reduce by 25%. There will be enough payroll taxes to continue to pay 75% of benefits to recipients. Knowing this, it is easy to see how tax rates in the future could be significantly higher than they are today. The last point to this tip is to not overlook the cost of healthcare in retirement. Fidelity Investments conducted a study and found that the average expense for a retired couple is $280,000. It is the one financial landmine that can quickly derail a successful retirement plan and it can't be overlooked.

Guaranteed Sources of Income in Retirement are Key. What sources of income will you have in retirement? Social Security, a pension, personal savings such as a 401(k), IRA, 403(b), Thrift Savings Plan, Roth IRA, Real Estate income, etc. Today we see that the responsibility for saving for retirement has shifted away from employer sponsored pension plans to plans that require the employee to contribute to their retirement such as the 401(K), 403(b) and Thrift Savings Plan. Traditional financial planning has taught us to maximize our retirement plan contributions to reduce current taxes and because we will be in a lower tax bracket when we retire. If you believe that taxes will be lower in the future, then this is a great strategy. The truth is, we don't know what taxes will be in the future. But if you believe that taxes could be higher in the future then creating tax free sources of income is important. A person's sources of guaranteed income in retirement include social security and pension plan (if you are fortunate to have one). For those that don't have a pension plan you can create your own personal pension by using a portion of your retirement assets to generate a guaranteed income. The important aspect of income planning is knowing your sources of income, your expenses in retirement and coordinating your income in a manner that provides the income needed for your lifetime on a guaranteed basis, minimizes taxes and provides the greatest benefit to your surviving spouse or heirs.

To learn more about these concepts be sure to go to my website: www.jpdcapitalmanagement.com or call Toll Free: 1-888-605-8363

John P. Dubots, MPA is a nationally recognized Financial Educator, Author, Speaker and Retirement Planner, whom you may have seen in Forbes and Fortune. Dubots is the Co-Author of *Giving Transforms You!* And *Retire Abundantly*. He regularly shares his financial wisdom and experience as an Educator and Speaker with many organizations, universities, through a series of Public Seminars, as well as a former Radio Host on KTIE AM 590 for *Retirement and Money Matters* now broadcast as a podcast through iTunes and other media channels. As the Founder and President of Dubots Capital Management, LLC, John and his team have been showing executives, professionals and business owners how to grow, preserve and pass-on their hard-earned wealth since 1991 by providing independent, client-first financial, retirement and estate planning solutions. His education includes a B.S. in Resource Economics and an MPA (master's in public administration) form the University of New Hampshire.

Investment Advisory Services offered through John P. Dubots Capital Management, LLC, CA License #0822923.

SHARON DUNCAN

One Retiring Mistake Can Cost A Bundle

Be sure you put your feet in the
right place, then stand firm.
—Abraham Lincoln

·············· TIPS ···············

1. <u>Retiring</u>—Turn your headlights on to drive in the dark. Have a solid, realistic Retiring Plan.
2. <u>Retiring</u>—Don't believe everything you hear. Follow good advice and ignore the rest.
3. <u>Retiring</u>—Retiring done right is life-changing. Avoid bad decisions and irreversible mistakes.

···

A way-too-common retiring story…

> *Bob threw the stack of papers down on the table. It was supposed to be one of the happiest days of Bob and Ann's lives, and yet, here they sat, angry and frustrated.*

They had been dreaming about their retirement for years. They thought they were all set. But now there were so many doggone decisions to be made. Nobody told them it would be so confusing.

Ann's dad got a party and a lifetime pension; that was pretty straight forward. Bob and Ann have ALL these important decisions to make. It's overwhelming.

Bob already knew that some of the decisions they were facing couldn't be changed. Once the form was signed and submitted, the choices can't be undone or changed. The HR department was NO help; they say they can't give advice. (Not that they have the relevant expertise anyway.) Bob and Ann talked with their financial advisor and now they had a pretty 50-page report. Their advisor told them the report said they would be fine and wasn't much help when it came to making many of the decisions Bob and Ann were facing.

They needed help.

I've heard some version of this story hundreds of times over the years.

Many people talk about saving *for* retirement. Others talk about *being* retired. However, the choices you make *in between* these two chapters in your life may be the most important choices you make for retirement, sometimes setting you on an irrevocable retirement lifestyle path.

It's the *retiring process*. Nobody is talking about the *retiring process*.

Retiring decisions may dramatically alter your retirement years—for good or for bad. According to the Social Security Administration[1], a 65-year-old will live 18-20 more years on average. "On average" means one half are still living after 20 years—2 out of 3 will live past age 90; and 1 out of 7 will live past age 95[2]. That means that you will need to replace your paycheck for 15, 20, 25, or even 30 or more years.

Their story continues...

> *Bob and Ann researched online. They bought three 5-star-rated books from Amazon. They attended two dinner seminars and met with the presenters, who sometimes just seemed to be pushing their one-size-fits-all financial product. They even asked family members, who had a plethora of opinions.*
>
> *Everyone has an opinion.*
>
> *But Bob and Ann don't want opinions. They want an established process, and wisdom from someone who is experienced at retiring. They don't want to blow it. This is their chance to set the course for their retirement.*
>
> *Ann knew they were in over their heads. They can't do it themselves.*

---

[1] Retirement & Survivors Benefits: Life Expectancy Calculator. www.SSA.gov July 2020.

Then a light bulb went off for Bob. His good friend, Jonathan, retired a few years ago and he was a company Controller. They talk from time to time and Jonathan said he went through a retiring process of some kind. Bob didn't pay attention at the time, since he was still a few years away from retiring, but now it was time to make a call about it.

Bob and Ann were discovering that the process of *retiring* is very different from saving for retirement. Not for amateurs. Not for generalists. Retiring, like anything complex and critical, requires a specialist with an established process. There are many decisions to be made and some of the decisions can never be changed, even if they turn out to be wrong decisions. Poor retiring decisions can be very costly.

Their story continues...

Jonathan had found an advisor specializing in retiring. He called them and they sent him a Retiring FITT® Scorecard and Special Report. Bob and Ann went through the scorecard and report.

The scorecard and report showed them that they needed help.

What questions should they ask? What if they were wrong about something? That's when tears started to roll down Ann's check. They have worked hard for this. They needed someone who could really help them.

They soon had an appointment with Jonathan's Retiring Specialist.

Retirement is an exciting dream we all have from the day our career starts.

Like Bob and Ann, you have probably done some planning along the way. If you are a successful saver, you have thought about what you'll do when you're retired.

Once you start taking a serious look at what you need to do to retire, you enter that place between saving for retirement and being retired. Retiring is a different world than saving for retirement. A world with many questions—hard questions.

Many questions... tough decisions... real life consequences. That's retiring. Good news—retiring doesn't have to be like driving at night without headlights.

Let's turn on the headlights...

Working through your 401(k), pension (if you have one), Social Security and health insurance decisions are where most people start. It's a good start but retiring is not this simple.

There are actually 25 different areas to consider when *retiring*.

The good news is that it doesn't have to be overwhelming and confusing. A well-tested *retiring process*, along with solid advice, can make a world of difference, helping you be sure you won't run out of money in your lifetime, getting everything you have coming to you, and making good decisions for your family.

This is NOT financial planning, which is a good tool for saving a nest egg for retirement. A *retiring process* is the next step beyond financial planning; comparing the advantages, disadvantages and results of one retiring choice versus another, and how different choices affect each other.

Bob and Ann had a typical financial plan done for them by an advisor that they had worked with for years. A typical financial planning process does not always deal with all the complex decisions required in *retiring*. It often leaves people feeling scared, overwhelmed and confused.

The foundation and driving force in the *retiring process* is a crystal-clear picture of your dreams and desires. Imagine you could go anywhere and do anything you wanted—what would you do?

Once you tune, and fine-tune, your dreams and desires for retirement, the *retiring process* systematically walks through the 25-retiring danger/opportunity areas to help you make the right decisions and help ensure that you and your money are protected and that you have taken advantage of the many retiring benefits available to you.

Their tale continues...

The Retiring Specialist they met with helped them clarify and discuss their goals and concerns.

They addressed the 25 different areas in their Retirement Roadmap in detail.

They worked together to lay out and address some specific, actionable steps to help them through the retiring process.

Having a process and plan in place can help to further reduce peoples' feelings of being scared, overwhelmed and confused.

As in any industry, not all advice is equal.

Financial licenses give someone the right to offer different financial products, services and solutions. Designations and certifications require training and testing. There are more than 200 designations available to financial professionals[3], each requiring different areas of knowledge, some focused on insurance products and planning, some on financial products and planning, some on investing, some on 401(k)s, etc.

Currently, there is no specific designation or certification for the *retiring process*. A good starting point is the combination of the CERTIFIED FINANCIAL PLANNER™ certification and active membership in Ed Slott's Master Elite IRA Advisor Group℠, who you may have seen on multiple PBS specials.

---

[3] FINRA, "Professional Designations." July 2020.

Designations and certifications are only a starting point. You've probably heard, "What do they call someone who graduates last in medical school? A doctor." Having a designation or certification does not necessarily equate to mastery. Becoming a seasoned advisor who specializes in the retiring process requires hundreds of hours of training, many years developing the real-world experience needed, and an ongoing effort to keep abreast of changes in retirement law, tax rules, financial solutions, regulations, etc.

Here are a few questions to ask:

- Are you an advisor specializing in retiring? Can you show me your Retiring Process and a sample plan?
- How many areas do you work through when you help someone through the *retiring process*?
- How many others have you taken through the retiring process and can I talk to three of them?

Warren Buffet said he wanted three things from his advisors: 1) Someone he can trust implicitly; 2) Someone who is at the top of their game professionally; and 3) Someone he enjoys spending time with.

Retiring mistakes can derail your retirement dreams and desires. Some permanently.

Retiring right can set you on a course of confidence, freedom and joy. We call it Retiring FITT®—Retiring for Today and Tomorrow. That's why we created the Retiring

FITT® Scorecard and Special Report. To get your copy and see where you stand, call us today at 281.990.7100 or go to www.SelahFS.com.

Retiring doesn't have to be scary, overwhelming and confusing, when it's done right.

The preceding is a hypothetical case study and is for illustrative purposes only. Actual performance and results will vary. Any resemblance to actual people or situations is purely coincidental. This case study does not constitute a recommendation as to the suitability of any investment for any person or persons having circumstances similar to those portrayed, and a financial advisor should be consulted.

Sharon Duncan, CFP®, AIF®, MBA, is a recognized Financial Educator, Author, Speaker and Creator of The Retiring FITT® System, a retiree-centered system created out of her frustration by financial myths and misinformation and the traditional "rollover your money and buy my product" process. She works on a national level to help retire families in a way that makes sense. Duncan's work has been published by *Yahoo!Finance, Houston Business Journal, The Houston Chronicle, Investor Business Daily, US News & World Report, and Wall Street Journal.* Duncan, the Founder of Selah Financial Services, was recognized on the Financial Times 400 Top Financial Advisers list in 2018.** Sharon is a member of Ed Slott's Master Elite IRA Advisor Group[SM*], as seen on PBS. Securities and advisory services offered through Commonwealth Financial Network®, Member FINRA/SIPC, a Registered Investment Advisor.

*Ed Slott's Master Elite IRA Advisor Group[SM] is a private IRA study group of professional financial advisors.

**To compile the 2018 list, the Financial Times evaluated nominees on six primary areas and calculated a numeric score for each advisor. The areas of consideration were assets under management (AUM), asset growth, compliance record, experience, credentials, and accessibility. Approximately 880 qualified applications were received; 400 advisors were selected, representing 45.4 percent of applicants. Not indicative of advisor's future performance. Your experience may vary. For the full methodology, please visit ft.com.

BRIAN GRAY & JOHN GOODHUE

Don't Miss Your Bucketlist Window

"Twenty years from now you will be more disappointed by the things that you didn't do than by the ones you did do. So, throw away the bowlines. Sail away from the safe harbor. Catch the trade winds in your sails. Explore, Dream. Discover."
—Mark Twain

••••••••••••• **TIPS** •••••••••••••

1. Don't miss your Bucket list Window
2. Spend your money safely without regret
3. Build your life resume

Definition: Bucket list (noun): The things you want to do, see and experience before you die.

Definition: Window (of Opportunity) (noun phrase): The time to act before it's too late.

Take your age and subtract it from 80. That is YOUR Bucket list Window. The window of opportunity that you have left in this life to do all the things on your bucket list. For most people their bucket list Window is about 15 years (80-65). Because after about age 80, life tends to turn your focus to health and healthcare and you just physically can't take the trips and do the other things you always wanted to do. That's not much time to fit in a lifetime of dreams and wishes about the things you want to experience before you meet your maker. Let's dig a little deeper into this idea so we can help you get out there and live your Bucket list Window to its fullest!

Doing your bucket list was the theme of the fantastic 2007 movie "The Bucket List" starring Jack Nicholson and Morgan Freeman in which two terminally ill patients set out on a road trip to check off as many things as they can on both of their bucket lists before they run out of time. It should be required viewing for everyone going into retirement. If you've seen it or not, we suggest you should watch it after you read this chapter. You might have a different perspective on its message.

But first things first. Do you have a bucket list? If not don't worry, we're going to help you get one started. If you do, then we're going to give you some tips that may help you fill it out more fully. Sit down in a quiet space with a blank piece of paper and maybe your favorite adult beverage and think of all the things you have dreamed about doing all of your life. DO NOT focus on the cost of any of these things because you don't want to put a limit on your dreams.

We see time and time again that if someone thinks it costs too much then they just won't do it. Savers hate spending money. And just as often, when we design their retirement plan, we show these same people that they can easily afford to do everything on their bucket list without any risk of running out of money or reducing the legacy they want to leave to their children and charities. If you have a significant other, then be sure to make your initial bucket list separately to start and then compare lists. You will probably find that you have a lot of things that you want to do in common and some things that you'll want to add to your joint list.

The next step is to prioritize the items that will require more physicality. You want to get these out of the way before you may need to get your knees and hips replaced. Prioritize each one based on your desire to get these items done so you won't have any regret if you don't. Once you prioritize your list it is now time to set specific goals so you will have a better chance of actually doing the things on your list.

You need to go deeper than saying "we will go to Italy". There is a lot to see in Italy. Say it like this, "We will leave for Italy on Saturday, June 15 next year. We will book our trip on November 20 of this year with ABC Tour Company. We will fly first class both ways and stay in only 4 star and better hotels. We will visit Rome, Florence, Lake Como and Venice spending 3 days in each location." Get the idea? Be specific about what you want to do while you're there. Do you want your trip to include museums, wine tastings, cooking classes? Self-guided or on a tour? Do you want to experience Italy by car, train or cruise ship? By setting specific goals you will most likely do more research, get excited and most importantly TAKE ACTION to start checking off the items on your bucket list.

We do find that even when people put their list together, that there are things that cause people to freeze and not achieve what they want. Fear, worry and life experiences tend to make people not finish their life strong. Instead, those people end life with a whimper and lots of regret. With proper planning you can feel more comfortable spending the money to achieve your dreams. It is imperative to have a real, honest to goodness, written plan so you absolutely, positively know without question or doubt that you can do the things on your bucket list and feel free to live the rest of your life without limits or boundaries.

The alternative is not something we wish for you. In meeting with thousands of people over the years to help with their retirement planning, we have often heard from people in their 80s "We wish we had spent more of our money in our 60s and 70s when we were healthy, because now we can't travel or do the things we always dreamed of doing." Too many people put off living their lifetime dreams until "tomorrow", the day that never comes. Ultimately their health finally fails them, and their lifetime dreams end up staying on a piece of paper, never becoming reality.

> "Twenty years from now you will be more disappointed by the things that you didn't do than by the ones you did do. So, throw off the bowlines. Sail away from the safe harbor. Catch the trade winds in your sails."
>
> —Mark Twain

Now that you have a better idea of what your bucket list should look like, we want to discuss what we call "Living Life in Five Year Increments". When people think of retirement, they generally think they have 25 to 30 years left to get everything they want to do done. But how does life really work? When you look at your bucket list you will find that you have some big things, some middle size things and some small things that you really want to do. As we noted at the start of this chapter, when you retire at about age 65 you have about 15 good years left until health and healthcare concerns rule your life.

You should start doing the big things on your bucket list in the first five years from age 65 to 70 while you are still healthy. After all, Europe and South America were not made for wheelchairs, walkers and canes. These are your "Go, Go Years" of retirement. About age 70 to 75 you may still be doing some of the big things on your bucket list, but we bet you will transition to doing more of the midsized things. We call these the "Slow Go Years" in your retirement. And by the time you reach your 80s you will probably be focusing mainly on your health and healthcare. These are your "No Go Years".

Now, don't get us wrong, your Slow Go Years can still be amazing years. With the spiraling advances in healthcare, it's not doubt that we are living longer and better lives. However, most people in their 80s are not able to travel the world and hike mountains anymore. That's why it is so important to get the big and midsized things on your bucket list done when you're still young enough to do and enjoy them. If you don't, regret about what you didn't do will likely be part of your retirement. Plan now so you don't regret later. And definitely don't let the day you die be the day your kids retire... and spend all the money that you didn't use to fulfill your lifetime of bucket list dreams.

We want to end this chapter with one of our favorite bucket list item stories. Joan's family is everything to her, so she has found an amazing way to enjoy time with her family. Every three years, Joan rents a luxurious home in Southern California and pays for all of her children, their spouses and her eight grandchildren to come out for a two-week visit. Joan pays for all the expenses, so the family doesn't have to worry about a dime. Now, this does cost a pretty penny, but Joan tells us every time that the memories and experiences she creates, and more importantly, her children and grandchildren create and share with her about their trips to California with mom and grandma are truly priceless.

So, don't miss your Bucket list Window. You truly only have one chance at getting this right. Get your bucket list ready. Start planning your first big bucket list experience. Remember to get down in the weeds with your planning. Don't just say "We're going to Italy". Then once you've done one, get to doing number two, then number three, and don't stop until you can't physically do it anymore. Here's to truly living your retirement.

BRIAN GRAY AND **JOHN GOODHUE** are nationally recognized Educators, Authors, Speakers, and Wealth Advisors, whom you may have seen on NBC, ABC, CBS and Fox network affiliates and F*ortune, Money, Bloomberg Business, Market Watch, Wall Street Select, Denver Business Journal,* and others. As Co-Authors of Giving Transforms You, Co-Creators of *The Smiling Through Retirement Process*™ and Co-Founders of APO Financial, they have been interviewed by Kevin Harrington, original *Shark* on the multi **EMMY**® Award winning TV series, *Shark Tank*, and by James Malinchak, featured on ABC TV's Hit Series, *Secret Millionaire*. They have also interviewed such notables as Country Music star Martina McBride and renowned economist Roger Ibbotson. At APO Financial, John, Brian and their team show executives, professionals, business owners, and women on their own how to safely grow, protect and spend their hard-earned money, so that their clients can enjoy their future with the people and things they love.

DAN HAGLER

The One Critical Factor to Retire AND Stay Retired

If you can't describe what you are doing as a process, you don't know what you're doing.
—W. Edwards Deming

••••••••••••••• TIPS ••••••••••••••

1. Work with a fiduciary; they're in the same boat rowing with you.
2. Have a written plan and test it annually; it could save your financial life and legacy.
3. Avoid the assembly line financial planning.

••••••••••••••••••••••••••••••••

Jack Desmond, a very successful Fortune 100 executive, prided himself on always being in total control while he was working.

"Jack, you seem unusually tense," Ted Walters remarked to Jack, five years his junior.

"Amanda and I are fussing over money again," Jack confided.

Then the dam let loose.

Jack went on a tirade in machine-gun fashion, "She wants to fix up the house AND keep traveling. You know, see the grandkids, vacation in Europe, see where her grandparents were born in Italy. I promised we would, but I'm nervous. You know, the market's been sideways and we're due for another correction… or crash…or whatever they call it now. My parent's health is not good, and they are barely surviving on social security. Plus, we're helping the kids out. It has gotten me a little worried. Sometimes I wonder whether I might have to go back to work at some time."

Ted remarked, "Wow. I thought you were in good shape financially."

"Me too. I mean we are, sure," Jack responded. "Our advisor keeps telling me everything is OK. Am I supposed to just take his word? So many uncertainties. Truth is, I'm not so sure. Can you really know with all the uncertainty in the economy and the world?"

"Sure can," Ted replied.

"C'mon. Really? How?" Jack wanted to know.

"One thing," Ted answered, "simulation."

"Simulation?" Jack inquired.

"Think about when you were in charge of the North American division. Did you ever make a business decision without having your team run simulations?" Ted asked.

Jack said, "Of course not."

"As president, I always had our CFO running simulations. That's what gave me the confidence to make decisions. Who's running your retirement simulations," Ted asked with that intensity that only he could pull off.

Jack cocked his head and looked out the window.

Ted continued, "No wonder you're nervous. Right after I retired, I went to this private briefing on reducing income and estate taxes. It was there that I learned, like planning a business decision, or planning an airline flight, you must simulate multiple futures to determine the likelihood of success, as well as areas of vulnerability. Retirement is no different."

"I also discovered the 80 Percent Retirement Myth. How many times have you heard, *'You can retire on 80 percent of your final income,'*" Ted asked?

Jack replied still staring out the window, "Yea, I've heard that often."

"Has it been true for you and Amanda?" Ted probed.

Jack was now looking right at Ted, "Haha. No, actually our lifestyle has increased since I retired."

"Me too," Ted continued, "Think about it. When you were working, were there things you and Amanda wanted to do that you put off until retirement, and promised yourselves that you would do it once you retired?"

Jack nodded yes.

"Did you promise yourself that you'd spend more time traveling? More time going out to eat? More time playing golf?" asked Ted smiling. "Now you're nervous that you might run out of money. It's stealing your joy, isn't it?"

"Can't I just create an Excel spreadsheet and calculate it myself?" Jack asked.

"C'mon Jack," Ted shot back. "Did you just 'create an Excel spreadsheet' at the company? Do-it-yourself only works on TV."

Jack hated when Ted was right, so he gave him that look and said, "Of course not. Too many variables that are missed without someone who has training and years of black-top experience. And too much on the line."

"Having a customized retirement and lifestyle simulation and written plan of action gives Margie and me peace of mind. And freedom to enjoy our lifestyle without pinching pennies." Ted continued, "It helps us answer one of the most important questions, 'Can we enjoy the kind of lifestyle we want and have sacrificed for, even when the markets and economy are going up and DOWN?'"

Ted summed up, "The value of the simulation is not in trying to predict the future. It is seeking to understand the probability of success. And it identifies the factors that will increase or decrease your success. In a nutshell, it's the freedom to enjoy the lifestyle we want and do the things we want to do without freaking out every time the market goes down. And the freedom to turn off the financial news!"

Jack asked, "What happens if you don't like the *likelihood of success*?"

"Good question." Ted replied. "You can simulate different changes, either lifestyle or investing, then decide what you want to do. The trick is to take the least amount of investment risk you need to enjoy the things you want."

"Well, how has it helped you?" Jack challenged.

Ted thought for a moment and said, "It's allowed me to keep my promises. To Margie. And to myself. I'm not worrying about it in the middle of the night. Our retirement specialist regularly simulates the ups, **and the downs**, of the economy and the market. It gives me an ongoing peace that we are on the right path. Using it, they designed a lifestyle and legacy plan for us initially. Now we use it to make ongoing strategic adjustments. It's like having Google maps tell you to adjust your route to miss traffic and stay on the best path."

Ted continued, "C'mon over after and I'll show you our plan and simulation. Margie and I go through this at least once a year. Or when something unusual pops up. Every possible concern we have gets answered. I have more confidence about the future... and I'm playing better golf."

Ted was on a roll now, "The other day I read an article that said that less than a third of all Americans have an actual goal in mind for their retirement—and only a small percentage of them have any strategy for reaching that goal. On a day-to-day basis, the ups and downs in the economy and financial markets used to freak me out. You know, I was glued to the financial news, checking it out everywhere I went. Now, we have a strategic framework and pre-determined response plan when they *do* occur."

"Makes sense," Jack replied.

"Best of all, frankly, it's helped our marriage. Margie likes me more. Used to be, when we'd go out to eat, I would pressure Margie to get something cheaper," Ted shared. "Truthfully, I was a pain on vacation or when we'd travel. Always moaning about spending too much money. Now I have the confidence to get what we want. Maybe I like me more."

"Hmmm. Sounds interesting," said Jack.

Ted said, "Best place to start is an assessment of where you are. Our guy has a 17-Point Wealth Assessment. It pointed out things I wasn't even aware of. And I thought we were in pretty good shape. It's super helpful. You want me to recommend you to him?"

"We need to do something," said Jack.

Six months later...

Jack's phone buzzed. *"Hey Jack, golf Saturday?"*

He texted Ted back, *"Thanks but we're heading on vacation for two weeks."*

Almost instantly, Jack's phone starts ringing.

"Hey, Ted, what's up?" Jack asked.

"Two weeks? Where are you going?" Ted wondered.

"Italy, France and Ireland. And I'm playing Ballybunion and Killarney when we're there," Jack said, clearly gloating.

Ted asked, "Two weeks in Europe and golf. Wow! I thought you were freaked out about spending any more money?"

Jack shared, "Well. You were right. We met with your guy and went through the 17-Point Assessment. Super helpful. It uncovered some things I hadn't even thought about. Some opportunities to lower our taxes and increase our lifestyle, and some issues. I really like him. We decided to go through The Protected Retirement Process, like you did, and get a custom lifestyle and legacy plan."

"Good for you and Amanda. BUT... I am jealous of the golf part. I'm adding that to my plan," Ted said. "Text me pics, will you?"

To discover where you stand and what your dangers and opportunities are, schedule a 17-Point Wealth Assessment by calling 603-472-4447 or going to www.TheProtectedRetirementProcess.com.

Dan Hagler, CFP®, AEP® is a recognized **Financial Educator, Author, Speaker, Tax and Retirement Income Specialist**, whom you may have seen in CBS, ABC, NBC, Fox local affiliates and *Yahoo Finance, The Wall Street Journal's MarketWatch, Reuters, Boston Business Journal, Wall Street Select, New Hampshire Union Leader* and *Business NH Magazine*. Hagler is the Creator of The Protected Retirement Process®, Contributing Author of Retire Abundantly, Founder and CEO of Granite State Retirement Planning, Inc., and Continuing Education Instructor, who has instructed attorneys, accountants, and financial planners in advanced tax reduction, retirement and estate planning. Dan and his wife, Kristen, enjoy their three daughters, outdoor activities, and time at church in Goffstown.

GREG HAMMOND

Create a Clear Path to Purposeful Living

"I've learned that, yes, wealth is a tool that gives you choices—but it can't compensate for a life not fully lived, and it certainly can't create a sense of peace within you."
—Oprah Winfrey

•••••••••••••• **TIPS** ••••••••••••••

1. Build wealth around a purpose that means more to you than money.

2. Investing peace of mind is to know what you are invested in, and why.

3. Facing what holds you back from financial success—your 'money demons' is the difference between finances being your tormentor, or finances that empower you.

Money doesn't make people happy. Yet, most financial advisors begin a conversation about building wealth by asking how much money you have, and how much you want to have. At Hammond Iles we approach it differently. We begin with a purpose that is greater than money. Then we have fun exploring how to plan and invest toward that purpose.

We all have dreams, and many of those dreams rely on financial success to become a reality. When you think about your life, what is worth years of hard work, saving, and prudent investing? What exactly are you saving and investing for? Once we understand your true purpose for money, it can serve as a compass for all of your financial decisions.

A successful investing experience is about more than creating efficient portfolios. It is also about educating and empowering people so they gain a new level of confidence around money and investing and lay a foundation for future financial well-being.

Explore Your True Purpose Like There is No Tomorrow

If your life was over today, what would it take for you to say, "I have lived a life without regret?" What kind of relationships would you have had? What would you have experienced? What would your health and spiritual well-being be like? What impact would you like to have on the people, causes and organizations you care about? Dedicate some time to reflect on what you hope to accomplish while you are on this earth, and how you would like to be remembered at the end of your journey. Write down whatever comes to mind. Initially, don't worry about constraints such as time or money.

Unleash your imagination and awaken your dreams. Allow yourself to think bigger than you ever have before.

Once you make an initial list, take a break. Put your list aside. Allow your mind and subconscious to think and work on it. After a day or two come back to your list and review it. Did you think of anything new to add? Does something you initially wrote down not carry the same appeal it did when you first thought of it? Take time to get really clear on what you want to accomplish with your money and your life. This exploration could take just two sessions or it might take several. Keep repeating the review and think cycle until you feel good about your list. Remember, your list does not need to be complete or perfect. It can be changed at any time.

There are no right ways to work on this exercise and no wrong answers. Some people jot down a few key ideas or accomplishments and want to move on. Others keep their list handy in a journal or on their phone so they can reflect on it. No matter where you fall on the spectrum, this is one of the most important things you can ever do to design your future.

Once your list of life and money successes is complete, see if you can write a sentence or two about what you want your money to do, and what you would like your life to be like. This brief description reveals your true purpose for your money. In most cases, this is also your true purpose for life. You might find it difficult to sum up everything you want to do in only a sentence or several phrases. If you find it hard to come up with your overall purpose, you might find it helpful to talk with a purpose-focused financial coach. It can sound like an overwhelming goal, but going through this process can truly help you discover and name your true purpose.

"Believe in the kind of life you want, and go for it with all your heart."

When you consider your true purpose, decisions around the use of your time, money and energy become easier to make. If something is not in line with your purpose then you should pass on it and say "no" in order to continue on the path to the kind of life you aspire to live. Without a true purpose for money, no amount of wealth will ever be enough. Yet, once you discover your true purpose for your money, substantial wealth is not needed.

Without a purpose for money it is easy to become trapped in a cycle of stress, uncertainty and a lack of fulfillment. This cycle begins with concerns about surviving. Will I have enough? Will I outlive my money? Then something catches your eye: a car, home, clothing, travel, or something else you want. Despite your concerns about survival, you buy it thinking it will bring you happiness and joy. Enjoying your new item gives you a sense of satisfaction, relief, or exuberance—at least for a little while. However, after the newness wears off, you begin to compare your item with others around you. You see a newer model, a better color, a different style. Your neighbor, friend, coworker, or relative has a "better" one. And the cycle starts all over again with your concerns and desires. Do I need a new one? Would my life be better with an upgrade? This endless loop leaves you unfulfilled and steals your joy. You can help break this cycle by identifying your true purpose for money. What can money buy? Why do I want it? If this purchase is not going to help bring me closer to my true purpose, should I buy it? These questions can help you align your money and purchases with your purpose. They will allow you to be grateful for what you have, to know what your wealth is for, and to live a life with greater peace, impact, and fulfillment.

Clearing the Path

Knowing the true purpose for your money will help you invest your wealth in alignment with what you want in life. Have you ever gone to the grocery store with a list and returned with a few extra items that caught your eye even though they were not on the list? Often these "extras" somehow end up in the cart and we return home with more than we intended to buy. This same scenario happens with investment portfolios. Often a friend, relative, acquaintance or financial salesperson may recommend a specific stock, mutual fund, strategy, investment or insurance product. At the time, the investment made complete sense and sounded like a good thing to add to your portfolio. Over the years, as these recommendations and suggestions accumulate you might find yourself with a "cart" of assorted investments, products and strategies that do not have a common purpose or focus. Do you know if all of the investments, strategies, and products in your portfolio work together? Or do they have side effects? Are they overlapping investments that increase your risk? It is important to take a close look at what is in your investment portfolio to determine the risk you are taking compared to other diversified portfolios. Do you understand what you own and why you own it? And most importantly, does the amount of risk in your portfolio prudently support your true purpose for money?

After determining your true purpose for money and analyzing your current investment portfolio allocation and risk, the next step is to create a clear financial path from your current portfolio to a life of purpose. One of the best ways to do this is to work with a purpose-focused wealth advisor or financial coach. Working with a financial coach is like using the GPS in your car or smartphone. Once you determine your destination (your purpose), the GPS (your work with a financial coach) determines your current position and the best route to get you there. A thoughtful path avoids the stumbling blocks that can keep financial success beyond your reach.

Obstacles to Avoid and Be Aware Of

One of the biggest obstacles is one we commonly overlook—and most financial advisors never even discuss: Your personal beliefs about money. Throughout your life you have attached various meanings, values and stories to money. Whether you heard them from your parents, observed an adult's relationship with money, or acquired them from the media or culture, these subconscious beliefs and stories govern the way you think about and handle money. For many people, these beliefs are negative and become "money demons." These subconscious money demons steal your confidence and hold you back from taking command of your finances so you can reach for your dreams with knowledge and action that has the potential to transform your life and the lives of the people you care about. Many money demons center on scarcity or a lack of having enough. Perhaps you were told "Money doesn't grow on trees" or "Money is the source of all evil." With these thoughts of scarcity, you can't expect to attract and welcome more wealth into your life. Working with a financial coach to make you aware of these beliefs can help you create the future you imagine, feel confident about money, and worry less.

As with all things in life, it can be a challenge to stay on track. Thousands of years ago our human brain was wired for survival. Focusing on survival, your brain is always searching for potential dangers and ways to conserve energy. We have developed instincts, emotions and perceptions to assist with survival. While these brain functions are beneficial to your survival, they could be devastating to your wealth. For example, there are two basic instincts: pain and pleasure. Your brain will naturally try to move you away from pain and toward pleasure. These instincts work well if you are trying to avoid the pain of being attacked by a sabretooth tiger or have the pleasure of finding clear, cool drinking water, but they can cause havoc on your investment portfolio. If you open an investment account statement to find one investment increasing in value and another losing value, your instincts will cause you to want to sell the investment that is losing value (move away from pain) and buy more of the investment that is going up in value (move toward pleasure). But this can be disastrous for your wealth. You may have just captured a loss by selling the investment that was losing value only to invest in a higher priced investment and watch it start to go down in value. Following your instincts may cause you to change investments at the wrong time.

In addition, many advisors, financial companies, and the media try to take advantage of your instincts, emotions and perceptions. The media knows fear is a powerful emotion. This is one reason why negative headlines and stories are more prevalent in the news. Fear and concern will capture your attention. Listening to negative news on a regular basis will definitely impact your instincts, emotions and possibly your wealth. A single investment mistake can wipe out a lifetime of savings. Having a financial coach to make you aware of your instinctual behavior can help you avoid taking the wrong actions at the wrong time.

Unfortunately, the media is not the only outlet pouring out information that is not in your best interest. Many advisors and financial institutions create and distribute information to breed fear and confusion in order to increase business and pad their pockets. Just by its structure, Wall Street (and the financial system) is filled with transaction-based intermediaries who benefit when you buy and sell investments. They try to sell you a product so they can earn a commission, convince you they know where the financial markets are headed, and encourage you to make trades so they can receive fees. This gets your attention and makes you fearful.

As an investor, you need to be aware that the financial industry is a business. Wall Street and financial institutions earn a profit on your wealth. Just like the fast food industry has no interest in helping you maintain a healthy weight, most of the financial industry has no interest in helping you have a fulfilling life and enjoyable retirement.

Take the First Step

When you deepen your investing knowledge, slay your money demons, and align your money with your purpose, you will have the power to make informed choices about your financial future despite the obstacles you face. You can take command of your finances and reach for your dreams with knowledge and action that has the potential to transform your life and the lives of the people you care about.

But you must take the first step... Many people feel they need to reach a certain level of income or a specific net worth before they start to look at their true purpose or the impact they can make. But I tell every investor to start now! Even if this means taking an action in a very small way, it is time to start living the purpose you were created for. Live as the person you are inspired to be. One of my clients with limited wealth and a true purpose of 'generosity' started to make an impact on her community by volunteering and making small contributions to a charitable organization she wants to support. Another couple with a true purpose focused on their 'family.' They started to take their entire family on vacations to enjoy time with their children and grandchildren while creating memories they will remember forever.

Take time to think, dream and plan for the possibilities available to you now, as well as in the future. Life is too short not to do something that matters. Be generous. Enjoy life. Live out your purpose. Think about what you want your wealth to support and then partner with a financial coach to be your trailblazer for a clear path to purposeful living.

Today, you can begin to go after your dreams like your life depends upon it...

Three BIG Tips for Building Wealth Like a Shark:

Tip 1—Build wealth around a true purpose that means more to you than money.

Tip 2—Establish clarity and confidence around your investments by knowing what you are invested in and why.

Tip 3—Overcome the obstacles that hold you back from financial success—they are the difference between finances that torment you and finances that empower you.

Ready to Transform Your Financial Future?

You can get free resources and a schedule of special live events and webinars to help you learn about investing over a lifetime and how it can fulfill on your purpose for life at www.hammondiles.com. To get a better understanding of the risk and diversification in your investment portfolio and receive your personal Portfolio MRI® report, simply contact Hammond Iles Wealth Advisors at (800) 416-1655 or clientcare@hammondiles.com.

Greg Hammond, CFP®, CPA is a financial coach, author and speaker who is on a mission to make a positive impact in peoples' lives. As Chief Executive Officer of Hammond Iles Wealth Advisors, and co-founder of Planned Giving Strategies® Greg leads a team of professional financial coaches that educate and empower investors with the truth so they can make informed choices about their financial future.

As a recognized thought leader in the fields of wealth management and charitable giving, Greg helps people think differently about money and inspires them to design the kind of life they want to live. He freely shares his extensive personal and professional experience in business leadership and the financial complexities unique to entrepreneurs with others in the community.

From retirement planning, to succession planning, and implementing a donor's philanthropic plan, Greg brings with him a breadth of knowledge cultivated from over twenty years in investment management and financial services. Greg speaks at national conferences, estate planning councils, and religious and nonprofit organizations. Based on his book, *You Can Do More That Matters®*, he's been invited to appear on radio shows across the country. Greg co-hosted Planning for Tomorrow on CBS network WTIC News Talk 1080AM for over three years. He writes for The Street's Retirement Daily and has appeared in CNBC. com on the topic of "Succession Planning," the *Wall Street Journal* on "Earning Income" While Making a Gift, and the *Hartford Business Journal Nonprofit Notebook* for *Planned Giving.*

A graduate of Miami University with a B.A. in Accounting, Greg is a CERTIFIED FINANCIAL PLANNER™ Professional and Certified Public Accountant.

As an active philanthropist, Greg is well-known among nonprofit, faith-based, and charitable organizations for his generosity and advocacy on legacy giving. He supports the community through sponsorships, board, and committee involvement. Greg serves on the steering committee for the new Connecticut Children's Medical Center Infusion and Dialysis Centers. He and his business partner, Scott Iles host an annual fundraising event in support of the hospital.

Greg is an avid golfer and runner. He lives in West Hartford, Connecticut with his wife and two daughters.

www.hammondiles.com
www.domorethatmatters.com
Hammond Iles Wealth Advisors
100 Great Meadow Rd. Suite 701
Wethersfield, CT 06109
(800) 416-1655

www.hammondiles.comAdvisory Services offered through Hammond Iles Wealth Advisors. Securities offered through Ceros Financial Services, Inc., Member FINRA/SIPC (Not affiliated with Hammond Iles Wealth Advisors).

TIM HANSEN

Live Today for the Future

I skate to where the puck is going to be, not where it has been.
— Wayne Gretzky

••••••••••••• **TIPS** •••••••••••••

1. Invest in Yourself and Others
2. Expect the unexpected
3. Compound your Decisions

••••••••••••••••••••••••••••••••

Expect the Unexpected

I am a naturally optimistic person. The glass is half full! This perspective has helped me get through many challenges over the years. Looking on the bright side can frame things in an inviting way that has you facing a challenge rather than steering away. Many financial decisions get stalled by indifference or succumb to fear of the unknown.

A positive perspective helps when life throws something at you that you did not expect. Optimism gives you the energy to work through it. Unexpected events are also easier to deal with when you embrace the fact that you cannot predict the future, but you can prepare for it. And you can prepare by being aware of the possibilities in as many situations as possible. To help build that awareness, I created a four-step process called the IWBA Formula:

Step 1: Ask, "What **If**?" questions: What if I do? What if I don't?

Step 2: Then ask, "What's the **Worst** that could happen?" in each situation.

Step 3: Followed by, "What's the **Best** possible outcome from this situation?"

Step 4: Finally, "What **Action** will I take?"

Asking these simple questions forces your mind to work through what *could* happen and in doing so you naturally begin to plan what you might do if that scenario occurs. It's really about focusing on the result you seek. I have helped business owners deal with various situations and although we don't know the result ahead of time, we do know the preferred route.

Deciding whether to sell your business can feel like one of the most challenging questions you'll ever face. Your business is often related to your identity—without your business, something would be missing. Ultimately, though, you must make this decision at some point, or it will be made for you, unexpectedly. Here is an example of how my four-step process can help you figure out what you would do if you received an unexpected offer to sell:

Step 1: What if I **do** sell my business? I won't have an income but will have the proceeds of the sale.

Step 2: What's the worst that could happen? I run out of money.

Step 3: What's the best possible outcome from this situation? I sell my business and it lives on beyond me. I have more money than I need from the sale and can use it to change my life and the lives of others. I can focus on other things, like family, community and having experiences I always wanted to have.

Step 4: What action will I take? I will minimize the chances of having the worst possible outcome by determining my financial needs.

Step 1: What if I **don't** sell my business? I continue to work, and life remains the same for now.

Step 2: What's the worst that could happen? I run out of the energy required to keep pace with my business and it begins to shrink. While doing that I miss out on other aspects of life that are important to me.

Step 3: What's the best possible outcome from this situation? I don't sell my business until I have a better offer, but I have no idea when that might happen.

Step 4: What action will I take? Set up a plan to protect my wealth.

The IWBA Formula preprograms your brain to be ready to act, just like a professional hockey player practising their slap shot over and over until it becomes automatic. Preparation takes the edge off the unexpected. It is hard to address every possibility, and some things truly do come out of nowhere, but you can minimize the negative effects on your life. Take control and be ready to act.

Here's an example: a recent decision our family made concerned purchasing a new home. We had a home, a great home—the one we lived in when our children were born. But the reality was, our family had grown, and we could use some extra room. Our parents are aging, and we cherish our time with them, but our house lacked some basic amenities for when they visited. The IWBA Formula led us to decide to sell, and we now find ourselves anticipating moving day in our new home. We are able to focus on the present and are back to enjoying special moments instead of stressing over what could be.

Invest in Yourself and Others

Practise personal development daily. Ask yourself, "What can I do today to get better and move closer to where I want to go?" That's a basic question that helps keep you on track towards your ultimate destination—always moving forward.

To understand where you need to invest in your development you must have a high degree of self-awareness. A multitude of assessments are available to help you figure out your strengths, blind spots, work style, communication style and personality. My favourites include the Myers-Briggs Type Indicator, StrengthsFinder, the Kolbe A Index, The 5 Love Languages and Achieving Authentic Success. The Myers-Briggs Type Indicator taught me I am an extravert, energized by the outside world, and I need people in order to stay invigorated. The StrengthsFinder tells me where I shine so I can leverage my strengths and minimize my blind spots. It highlights the path where I can excel and helps me communicate with others. Knowing your communication style helps you to understand how others communicate. Clear and constant communication can remove a lot of frustrations that can develop when you feel misunderstood. The ability to continually communicate well so you are heard is a key success factor.

I believe we live in a resource-rich world. The resources I am speaking of are books, podcasts, websites, software applications and the endless information available at our fingertips, literally, with the click of a button. I spend time every day doing something to improve my life. This learning has taught me to eat healthier, sleep differently, exercise consistently, be a better parent and spouse, build wealth and much more. It is a significant investment of time, but I know the results are worthwhile. An insatiable desire to learn benefits you greatly.

But there is only so much we can do on our own. Yes, you can grow, but your skill set is limited. As a business owner I need other people. The list of those I need is long and, depending on the situation, many different relationships may be required. I am talking about my family, friends, employees, members of my community, business partners and many more. I am often reminded of a time early in my career when I hired my first employee to help with the administrative side of my business. It was a big decision because my income was not where I wanted it to be, but I knew I needed to focus my energy on growing the business and I could not do both effectively.

A belief in someone who was able to bring a new perspective and skill set opened my eyes to how quickly I could advance my business with an investment in someone else. It was a risk, but it changed my path and I attribute much of today's success to that decision. Hiring my first employee was an experience that created an openness to having a team of professionals and mentors available to help deal with the many challenges of running a business. I am talking about accountants, lawyers, bankers, bookkeepers, personal coaches and more. It's all about strategic delegation—bringing in the experts to help you get there. I also think of the support I get from family and friends. It provides confidence and much-needed energy to get through obstacles and challenges.

Investing in others also means sharing the wisdom you have acquired along the way. Every generation is different from the last and it is important to pass wisdom on to make us all more successful. Yes, new challenges will arise, but we have left lots of challenges in the past. Buildings are bigger now, people live longer, we can produce more food, and in some cases, we have more wealth than we know what to do with—all evidence that wisdom has helped to make the world a better place. Share wisdom and invest in other people for a compounding effect on their results and yours.

Compound Your Decisions

I am sure you are aware of the impact that compound interest has on your money. What about the compound effects of your decisions? We make so many decisions in a day and it can be very taxing on our minds. Small decisions — everything from what we wear, what we eat for breakfast and what route we take to work — add up to frame how your day turns out; they compound just like interest. Every decision matters. We have all had days when we do not get out of bed when our alarms go off, we are late, so we rush choosing our clothing, maybe skip breakfast and take a "shortcut" only to be obstructed by roadwork. The result is generally not a good start to the day. Now take those simple decisions that created a poor start and repeat them three times a week. That turns into 13 days per month, 156 days per year and, over a 30-year career, 4,676 days with a rough start! How does that sound?

The most successful people have a secret sauce. They figure out what works and then repeat it. They focus on daily rituals and set in motion a series of good decisions: a heathy diet, good personal hygiene, daily exercise and structure in your day will create freedom, not the opposite, as some people believe. The freedom comes from not having to make as many decisions. As an example, several years ago, I decided to exercise three or four times a week. It seemed to work but the challenge was picking the day and what activity I would do. My success was tested regularly, and I often found a reason not to exercise. I now exercise daily, which eliminates the daily decision about exercising and makes it all about the activity. The results are a healthy body and an energized mind.

The challenge is making more right decisions than wrong. I don't think every decision can be perfect, but I do know that when you focus on making the best decision, which is not always the easiest one, the results are there to suggest we can win more than we lose.

Self-discipline is critical. Without it we can often take the easy route. The path of least resistance may not be the right path. I have already talked about the importance of others and when it comes to decision-making, having support helps immensely. Another set of eyes reduces the chance of making the less optimal decision. Then it is a just matter of your commitment to yourself and the impact you wish to have on your world.

When I consider the world, we live in and the challenges that lie ahead I can only focus on the tips I have learned along the way. I wake up every day and expect the unexpected. I am ready for it and it provides colour in my day. I invest time in my own development and invest in other people because investment in human capital is the greatest reward. I also realize that every decision matters, big or small. I am not afraid to make mistakes but look for more wins than losses. Wealth has many different forms but if I live today *for* the future, not in spite of it, I will grow wealth with those around me and finish strong by finishing together.

A Partner at Sutton Wealth Planning and CERTIFIED FINANCIAL PLANNER™ professional, Tim Hansen has been helping successful business owners, build, protect and pass on their wealth for over a decade. Tim is a recognized Financial Educator, Speaker and Mentor for entrepreneurs and business leaders.

Tim's passion for entrepreneurship started with humble beginnings in rural Saskatchewan, Canada. By age 10 he learned how to create profits raising animals for market and his drive for building wealth began. Tim's passion is helping successful entrepreneurs control their wealth and fulfill their dreams of authentic success. He knows for most ambitious entrepreneurs, wealth creation isn't the challenge, but when focused on growing their business, they are not in control of their personal wealth leading to confusion, fear and worry. Through a creative process, which Tim co-created, his clients instead achieve a unique impact, while enjoying lifestyle freedom and peace of mind about their wealth.

DON HARMELIN

Are You Overpaying Taxes to the IRS?

"There is nothing sinister in so arranging one's affairs as to keep taxes as low as possible."
—Justice Learner Hand

••••••••••••• TIPS ••••••••••••••

1. It's better to pay taxes on the seed, rather than on the harvest.

2. Irrevocable trusts can be quite flexible, when drafted by an expert.

3. When approached from a multi-generational perspective, retirement and estate planning becomes fun and exciting!

••••••••••••••••••••••••••••••

Are You Overpaying Taxes to the IRS?

If you want to continue making voluntary (non-deductible) donations to the IRS, read no further. If you want to avoid overpaying substantial taxes, read on.

Odds are most of you are unnecessarily overpaying capital gain taxes, income taxes when retired, and estate taxes.

Traditional retirement and estate planning do not address the biggest wealth planning fear faced by every affluent family—fear of the unknown. People fear the unknown...potential legal costs, investment fees, product commissions, and the biggest fear of all—fear of making the wrong decision. Successful, well-educated, and experienced in their respective career's, clients are often asked to make planning commitments before feeling sufficiently informed about their long-term side effects.

We often hear, "If I knew the right professional to guide me, I'd go see him/her." Or "I'm not sure if I know the right questions to ask of my advisors." If asked, most confess, "I don't want to spend time and money without knowing what I'll get in return."

Few individuals have the spare time or motivation to learn about creative and profitable tax-saving and asset-preservation strategies. But it's not your fault. After all, how many professional athletes make it to the Pros in more than one sport?

Today's fragmented legal, tax, and financial service communities are largely the reason for lost tax savings. The separation between responsibilities and expertise is what causes clients to unknowingly fall victim to the professional advisor divide. The type of assets, not just the amount, can make added tax savings possible.

Most people rely on the advice of a longtime CPA or attorney excluding other knowledgeable professionals. Tax planning for the affluent without a skilled insurance professional often proves incomplete. Although experts in their own fields, it's unrealistic to expect attorneys or CPAs to have that same level of expertise on insurance and annuity products.

People often come to our office thinking their financial, tax and legal affairs are all in good order. Some areas are in good order. But, if it were possible to save $100,000, $500,000 or even more than $1,000,000 in taxes, wouldn't you like to know someone who specializes in uncovering those missed tax savings?

We are educators and advocates for raising awareness of tax inefficiencies and unintended loss of family wealth. Several planning strategies can only be enhanced by including life insurance or annuities. However, if one is to enjoy the maximum tax savings available, the right products with the best contract features must be properly structured.

So, what ARE the results of thorough, cohesive planning?

You will pay lower income taxes, enjoy higher spendable income during retirement, and leave more wealth for your children and grandchildren when you are gone.

Most affluent individuals, even those who don't expect to pay estate taxes, think there is no way around paying high income taxes on their IRA upon death. But what if it were possible to eliminate income taxes on your IRA, would it be worth having a conversation? A 75-year-old retiree who became a client certainly thinks so. Before we met, his $1 million IRA would suffer an income tax cost of $400,000 (more than that amount in states like New York, Connecticut and California). We guided the gentleman in trading that unnecessary $400,000 income tax cost, for a $2,000,000 tax free benefit for his grandchildren. Delivering more than four times what his grandchildren would otherwise receive, can only be achieved, by including insurance products in his planning.

If you are a business owner with five or more years before retirement, would it be worth having a conversation to learn how it is possible to make income from your retirement savings tax-free—for the rest of your life? A 60-year-old entrepreneur is happy we had that conversation. He plans to retire at age 67 and looks forward to avoiding taxes on his retirement income. Our recommendation was especially attractive because, in his situation, no change is needed to his already planned yearly retirement saving amounts.

A stockbroker brought her client to me after attending one of my seminars on tax saving ideas. The client was a recently retired executive at a well-known public company, who owned a significant amount of employer stock. Normally, the sale of his $1 Million stock holdings would require payment of more than $200,000 in capital gain taxes. However, by following our strategy, he was able to avoid paying taxes on the sale and reinvest his full $1 Million. Had we not met for a conversation, it would have cost him over $200,000 in unnecessary taxes, which would have resulted in lower income during retirement.

The CPA handling my parents trusts for the past 15 years complimented me on the planning I had done for my parent's and asked me to help her firm with advanced planning for some of their key clients. Even though my father had done a great job of keeping his documents up to date (my father and grandfather were both in the insurance business), tax laws keep changing. Shortly after my father died, I was able to improve on his already good planning. My mother then received a 300% increase in yearly spendable income for the rest of her life. We were also able to protect her investment portfolio against stock market risk and guarantee a 200% increase in tax-free inheritance received by my three siblings and me.

An attorney sent me a client, who came to him to put together his will. During their conversation, the 36-year-old man expressed a desire for more insurance coverage for his young family and asked if he knew anyone in the industry. I received a call from the young man to discuss his needs and concerns, which included wanting to save more for retirement. Having received his MBA from Columbia University, I recognized his strong knowledge of investments and taxes, so I provided him with plenty of research material for his own review. Once we met, he shared with me that he felt that the strategy was not only extremely attractive, but safe as well. His analogy was: "it's kind of like going bowling and having bumpers on either side of the lane; you never end up with a gutter ball."

The tax partner of a CPA firm recently adopted my recommendation to use a specially designed insurance product, as an alternative retirement savings plan. Like the investment guy we spoke about earlier, who did his research and found it to be a great product, she did too. We were able to enhance her structure in different way, so that whatever premiums she paid, we could increase the value by 4x. The goal was to maximize her retirement income, and she recognized tax benefits available only through life insurance. Basically, she's paying 25c for the value of a dollar!

Concerned about an insurance policy he was sold three years before, a highly respected and well-known tax attorney contacted me. He told me, "Something didn't feel right. Every time I've asked for written information or asked for explanations to better understand what I bought, I got the run around or a lot of hype about how great a product he sold me, but I couldn't understand the guy." He had known the agent socially for close to 20 years, so he assumed he could trust him. He asked if I could review what he had bought and give him a second opinion.

Based on how the product had been described to him, the attorney bought the policy, paying over $1 Million during the first three years. After reviewing the policy and work completed by the agent, we realized that not only had the product been misrepresented, he didn't provide the buyer with required disclosures. Worst of all, the agent had forged the client's signature on multiple forms.

This was one of the most shocking violations of public trust by a life insurance agent I have ever witnessed. After spending six months analyzing sales illustrations and coaching the insured on what to say to the insurance company, a little more than a million dollars cash was recovered from the carrier without requiring legal action by my client. Thankfully, this misconduct is not the norm as it is not likely that many other policy reviews would result in refund of premiums already paid. Unlike many other insurance people, I am independent, representing my clients in the market, not a specific insurance company. This case is an example of our commitment to making sure insurance carriers treat our clients fairly.

The success of our office is based on the tangible and measurable results we deliver to clients, regardless of how much of time is required. That is why we follow a pre-engagement protocol before deciding to accept each new client. Every client situation is specific to their personal circumstances and our recommendations are custom tailored to meet their individual needs and objectives. We operate differently than a traditional fee-based business. We invest whatever time and research is required to deliver maximum value to each client. We are a result-based service, not fee based. If we have not delivered measurable financial and tax saving enhancements to a client's current family situation, we do not expect to be compensated.

My father started teaching me about life insurance before I was a teenager. Because I was force fed life insurance facts and information even though I wasn't sure what career I would choose after college, I was certain I was not going to sell life insurance! What I remember most from those weekly insurance sessions was how seriously my dad took his work. More than anything, he emphasized, "I consider myself a fiduciary, similar to what's expected of an attorney, even though I am paid by commission." He instilled in me his belief and commitment "to not worry about the commissions. Always do what's best for the client, and commissions will take care of themselves."

For more information, or to schedule a no obligation conversation with Don, he can be reached at: 203.352.2940 or don@wci-ct.com.

Don Harmelin, Founder of Wealth Consultants, Inc., has devoted more than 30 years advising successful business owners, highly compensated executives and high net worth families. The wisdom gained from more than 30 years of experience results in delivering custom solutions that protect, preserve and enhance family wealth—in ways affluent families had not previously imagined. Using interdisciplinary, prudent tax efficient strategies, Don's clients realize profits, when others realize costs. His clients realize living benefits from insurance products and enjoy higher spendable income during retirement. Don brings a unique perspective from a three-generation family tradition of more than 100 years in the life insurance and financial services profession.

A graduate of the University of Oregon, Don Harmelin, Chartered Life Underwriter (CLU) and Chartered Financial Consultant (ChFC), resides in Stamford, CT. In his free time, he enjoys swimming, tennis, and quality time with friends and family.

ERICA HERBST

The 3 Reasons to NEVER Invest in Real Estate

Ninety percent of all millionaires become so through owning real estate. More money has been made in real estate than in all industrial investments combined. The wise young man or wage earner of today invests his money in real estate.
—Andrew Carnegie

• • • • • • • • • • • • • • **TIPS** • • • • • • • • • • • • • •

1. "Start Small and Build It." —Kevin Harrington
2. Buy Real Estate in Up and Coming Neighborhoods.
3. Photos and Staging Matter, More Than Ever

• •

Real estate investment takes commitment, research and planning. If it is done right, it can be very lucrative and rewarding. However, it is not for everyone. Don't invest in real estate unless you are READY, WILLING and ABLE to ride it out for the long term.

Over the last two centuries, about 90 percent of the world's millionaires have become so by investing in real estate. If you want to build wealth, real estate investment is one of the fastest and safest ways to do so.

As Andrew Carnegie once said in his famous quote:

> Ninety percent of all millionaires become so through owning real estate. More money has been made in real estate than in all industrial investments combined. The wise young man or wage earner of today invests his money in real estate.
>
> —Andrew Carnegie

It sounds like a no-brainer to invest in real estate, doesn't it? Well, it's not for everyone and it's not a slam dunk way to get rich quick.

Never invest in real estate UNLESS you are able to:

1. Start with at least ONE property. You have to be in it to win it. If it's not the right time for you to buy a property, that's ok too.

> "Start small and build it."
>
> —Kevin Harrington

For the average investor, real estate offers the best way to develop significant wealth. When I am talking about real estate investing, I am referring to two different ways to go about it. The first is purchasing a property for the sole purpose of living there yourself, building equity and then trading up into your next home and so on and so forth. The second way is to invest in a rental property that generates cash flow from tenants.

Trading Up a Primary Residence

One of my clients, Ian, asked me recently, "Erica, why wouldn't you tell all your clients to invest the way I have? It's worked out so well for me and I would have never been able to afford my current home if it hadn't been for a good strategy on that first small condo purchase 7 years ago." Here's a little backstory on this: Ian purchased a small fixer-upper condo in an up-and-coming neighborhood and made smart decisions when he renovated that he knew would appeal to many buyers in that town. He asked for my advice on renovations and buyer likes and dislikes every step of the way and it was a very collaborative effort. I gave him ideas from local new construction model homes in the neighborhood when he was making his design choices. Builders usually have a large design budget for their model homes and know the hottest new trends, so I always advocate touring those homes in advance of the design updates in a home. Only a couple years later, that condo value doubled so he decided to upgrade to a 3 bedroom townhouse and replicated his smart design choices and again that home grew in value. The cycle continued as he upgraded, renovated and built up his equity, purchasing 4 homes in 7 years. Ian's real estate investment success all started with one small condo purchase.

Barbara Corcoran, founder of The Corcoran Group and a well-known and respected shark on "Shark Tank," started small and built from there.

"Buying real estate has made me rich—mostly through necessity, not by design. I bought my first itty-bitty studio after scraping together a few bucks because I needed to live somewhere anyway...Buying that tiny studio was the most important decision I made because it got me in the game."—[CNBC, "Real estate is still the best investment today, millionaires say." Oct 1, 2019.]

Rental Properties Will Bring Passive Cash Flow

Alternatively, you may want to invest in a rental property that is not your primary residence. One of the first questions you must ask yourself is, "What type of property do I want to purchase?" This first purchase should align with your investment goals and it is prudent to discuss your options with your trusted circle, including your financial advisor. Of course, many different factors will drive your overall investment strategy, but these five questions will help determine the types of properties you will consider as part of your real estate purchasing strategy:

1. Do you want to buy single-family homes?
2. Do you want to buy new construction homes or resale homes?
3. Do you want to buy condos?
4. Would you consider buying commercial properties or commercial/residential mixed use properties?
5. Do you want to purchase multi-family homes?

Following that, there are many factors to consider, including:

1. Knowing the costs involved with purchasing that particular property, including maintenance costs, utility payments, taxes, and budgeting for upgrades.

2. Location is key. Do your research on competing properties and know your numbers on what the rental property can yield. Know the community and key points that will attract potential renters to your unit.

3. Inspect before you buy. Hire the right inspector to perform a thorough inspection of the property so you are aware of any potential major issues upfront.

4. Surround yourself with a tribe of trusted people who want to see you succeed. You will likely need a real estate broker, an attorney, a CPA, lender and property managers. Additionally, you will need the right contractors to do your maintenance work and keep your asset in good working condition.

5. Know your numbers to protect your investment.

When done properly, real estate investment can be lucrative. It starts with ONE new property and, if done correctly, the possibilities are endless.

Never invest in real estate UNLESS you are able to:

2. Have a long term perspective to weather ups and downs.

Investing in real estate takes time, patience, and more patience! Do you have the willingness to endure over the long term?

Although sometimes real estate properties will lose value, over the long term they will almost always increase in value. If there is a loan on the property, over time the loan amount will decrease because it is being paid down, thus building equity.

"Investing in real estate is a great idea if you are in it for the long haul, not a quick return," says Bethenny Frankel, entrepreneur, and founder of Skinnygirl and BStrong. [CNBC, "Real estate is still the best investment today, millionaires say." Oct 1, 2019

"The only people who lose money in real estate are those who bought at the height of the market and sold at the wrong time or took too much equity out of their home, leaving no profit margin when they sold it. It often takes time to see big appreciations, but if you hold on to your investment, you will," says Dottie Herman, CEO of Douglas Elliman. [CNBC, "Real estate is still the best investment today, millionaires say." Oct 1, 2019.]

Real estate investments carry less risk than the stock market, where there are many uncontrollable factors. Those who have patience in investing long term in this tangible asset will reap the rewards and be positioned well to build wealth through real estate.

Never invest in real estate UNLESS you are able to:

3. Have a "Stacking" mentality. Stack your income or recurring revenue by continuously buying properties.

Banks and lenders will allow you to borrow against the equity in your home. You will build equity in the first property and then refinance and use that cash for the down payment on the second property. That second property will appreciate while you pay down the mortgage and you are building equity again. And again. And then again. This can create a second income or total income replacement for you. When you stack, not only are you creating cash flow but you are gaining experience and knowledge of the market. You are getting smarter; therefore, making more prudent decisions that will benefit you and your wealth strategy.

When you stack you can focus on creating S.T.A.R.S

- START with one property
- TACKLE the renovations efficiently
- ATTRACT the ideal tenant for the property
- REFINANCE so you can pull out cash for the next down payment
- START over!

See, you don't need to purchase a 100 unit apartment complex right off the bat. Stacking can start with purchasing only ONE property.

Do you have what it takes to invest in real estate as part of your mission to build wealth like a shark? Are you able to purchase that ONE property that will propel you forward? Do you have the time and patience to ride it out for the long term? And can you shift your mindset to stack and create your S.T.A.R.S.? If you answered yes to all three, you are positioned well to explore real estate investing further.

If you'd like to explore this topic or any real estate related topics in further detail, I have a collection of short videos and helpful articles I'd love to share with you. I encourage you to follow me on Instagram @e_key_realty and Facebook @eKeyRealtyInc to keep a pulse on current real estate trends and market updates.

As the founder of E KEY Realty, **Erica Herbst** leads a dynamic real estate team. Her influence is apparent with her "5-star Referral Center," providing clients and business owners Black Belt service.

Erica holds an MBA from the prestigious NYU Stern School of Business where she sparked her entrepreneurial mindset. Since then, she has invested in nationally prominent coaches to support her mission to lead, guide and protect her trusted clients, partners and friends.

Erica always had the passion to succeed. In college, she earned All-American Soccer honors and won a Women's Lacrosse National Championship at The College of New Jersey (TCNJ). In recent years, she discovered a passion for the martial arts and earned her Black Belt degree in Kyokushin karate.

Together with her daughter, Alexa, Erica wants to impact young women by coaching them to succeed in self-defense situations and developing their inner strength to succeed in life.

DAN HUNT

Top Mistakes Advisors Make and How to Avoid Them

·············· **TIPS** ··············

1. Falling for too-good-to-be-true lead and marketing programs
2. Chasing better returns, lower fees or both
3. Becoming too transactional
4. Neglecting to look and act the part
5. Operating as a lone wolf
6. Selling your business
7. Believing what got you here will provide future exponential growth

·································

Because I believe it is critical to understand how we got somewhere before we can exponentially grow, I'll give you the shortened version of what started me on the path that I am still on.

My mother was the female version of Warren Buffet in that she believed in buying as much of a company's stock that you can afford and never selling it. I recall her broker calling her repeatedly, begging her to sell everything during that week in 1987 when the market crashed but she refused. A few months later, her portfolio was like nothing ever happened. Fast forward to 1997. The market was revving up as the dot com wave was gaining steam, my full-time job in technology was going very well, and the family was growing with the recent birth of my second son.

Then my mom called with the worst news I have ever received. Two years later she was gone.

I was the executor of her estate, a tranche of mostly liquid assets not protected by a trust, ready to be taxed and spent. All of those decades of incredible investment discipline were gone instantly. I was the very person advisors and brokers loath. For no good reason at all, I moved it all, risked it all, and almost lost it all until a hand reached out and snatched me out of the quicksand. It was a stranger's hand and that stranger led me to a life and health license in 2004. The timing was perfect. The market had just crashed so selling asset protection was like shooting fish in a barrel.

Falling for too-good-to-be-true lead and marketing programs

If you have been independent in this industry for any length of time, you know exactly what I am referring to. We hear a new incredible lead generation story and we believe this marketing shortcut can lead us to substantial new clients. It costs us a few hundred or thousand dollars sporadically, with payments that are small enough that we feel comfortable paying, until we get sucked deeper into the abyss. Folks, that's how they do it! They take small bites that are just enough to make themselves money while not killing your business too fast.

The Advisor Shortcut Syndrome catches a lot of us. For those of us lucky enough to survive, we have undoubtedly moved into a marketing strategy that is much more realistic, albeit more expensive. There are marketing strategies that work very well, but you must prepare mentally, physically, and financially to grow into them.

The action item here is to lay out all marketing you do on a piece of paper, what it costs per month or year or lead, what each has produced, and typical business plan statistics. If it's not close to what you want or expect, throw it all away and start from scratch with a real plan. Our Advisor Transition Blueprint is a good read to begin anew and from there I can point you to resources to get you on the right track.

Chasing better returns, lower fees or both

Recall that I said to find out how to differentiate yourself from those around you? This is a great place to start. I can spot advisors who are real competitors and others whose process for determining value are misplaced or worse. Focusing on returns, fees, and a myriad of other statistics can easily get us in a position of weakness. We don't see this during a prolonged bull market when everything seems to be working everywhere. However, when the machine breaks down and all those stories, promises, processes, and products that you sold will come back for reckoning.

Our platform has been dealing in the ERISA (retirement plans) space for years. This is an environment that saw fee compression to the extreme; lawsuits have been initiated purely based on one fund's fees being a little higher than another fund in the same asset category. With this in mind, many retirement plan advisors and providers are sensitive to what can happen in the world of fees.

However, that does not mean that the service for managing a fund lineup (essentially what advisors do with retirees) needs to be free. There simply needs to be a well-documented and followed process. Fees can be fair if the process is good.

Returns are another benefit that advisors chase all the time, which can lead to all kinds of problems. Again, these problems don't occur on a day when the sun is shining but when there are high winds, lightning and rain. Advisors who over-sold returns will face the equivalent of running blind-folded, backwards, at night, and during a hailstorm. No wonder they tend to dodge client calls when things get tough.

Becoming too transactional

Advisors that have operated in the wire house arena for many years typically maintain solid client relationships. The book of business is valuable to both the advisor and parent company, so incentives are aligned to keep clients satisfied. Insurance agents operating as planners or advisors can fall into the transactional trap where, after years of good sales volume, they may not really know very many of their clients. If the agent wants to expand into offering Investment Advisor services an ideal way to get started is to approach every insurance client with a new and exciting integrated service offering. You would be surprised to learn how many insurance agents and brokers we've approached with this idea that have not moved forward for various reasons. When I first became an IAR I could not wait to call every single client we had to move them to this next level of service. It worked better than I expected, and it can for you as well. So, if you find you don't know very many of your clients, make that your top priority. Go out and shake hands with them or hold a nice event to get to know them again. If you fix this, you can then enhance your business by adding recurring services such as investment advice and financial planning.

Neglecting to look and act the part

Could you imagine going to a custom suit shop and the tailor is wearing sweatpants? Would you hire a personal trainer that was out of shape? Similarly, how many annuities do you own? How much of your own money resides inside the managed portfolios you are selling or even in the market? Everyone asks me, "What does a fiduciary really do?" I think our industry has gone off the deep end on this subject and suddenly everyone's a fiduciary. It has gone so far off the rails that you can apply for a fiduciary credential, having no securities or investment advisory license at all.

All that aside, actions are all that really matter. I think that true fiduciary behavior is a combination of two primary actions: 1) providing for what clients, individuals, families, or business owners really need, and 2) providing for what your own family, employees, and business really need. This means you will be leading by example, the trait I look for in any professional I work with.

For example, how can you tell a family they need principal protection when your family has none? Take the leap and practice the strategies you are selling. In the early days, I was living outside and below the image I was attempting to convey. Once I decided to really live and act the part, things got so good, I termed the experience "Expotential." Anyone can do it; it just takes the commitment.

Operating as a lone wolf

This job is difficult to do properly by yourself. If you are the chef, server, and dishwasher, your restaurant will likely fail. It is ironic that as advisors we are trying to grow and protect our client's financial assets while we simultaneously spend as little as we can growing our businesses. We end up doing everything ourselves, driving all over the country, and spending little time with family and friends.

Thankfully, I learned this facet of this business early on. To give you an example, we use an indicator we created long ago called, "investor personality." The purpose was to triangulate data (risk questionnaire and existing portfolio statistics) with the human personality we learn by interacting with the client. There are many ways to do this, and many tools to use, but we had our own formula. To give you an example, if someone shows you a portfolio that's been very conservative in target date funds for 20 years and they score 'maximum aggressive' on your risk test, could it be there's a personality mismatch? You bet there is!

This is also true with me. I discovered that when it came to servicing, nurturing, and responding to clients' needs, I didn't get excited about that at all. Let's say half of you are nurturers and the other half are hunters. Regardless of which side you are on, many clients need the ongoing support from both sides. If by your own personality you cannot or will not do it, that's an opportunity to fix. When I implemented a front-end support service (at our shared executive suite in those days), our growth trajectory changed for the better.

Selling your business

If you are 70 years old and have a succession plan in place, then you have done it right! If you are 37, have a great book of business, and a check for a few million looks enticing, you are not alone. I cannot say emphatically enough, "avoid the temptation for quick windfalls." Entering deals like this will give you a short term feeling of euphoria with a high probability of something going wrong in the coming years. The only way I could rationalize this approach is if either you are in a desperate financial situation or the pressure of controlling your own business is too much. It could be that this temporary fix will work but I would urge you to step back, weigh out all the benefits you hope to gain, and talk to peers who have done this before. Even better, get a business coach to help you assess such a decision.

Believing what got you here will provide future exponential growth

This one is my favorite. Like many of you I have been a victim of incorrect assessment. Reeling from the pain of too many horrendous decisions after I left my full-time employment, I was determined to find a path and stay on it. So that I would not get too out in front of my skis, I decided to go slow in what felt like an organic growth trance. You find a rhythm and stick with it, even if it means nothing big or significant seems to happen. Some people liken it to risk avoidance. While that could be part of it, I believed my personality as a risk taker could not be allowed to take over. For me, the attitude was to maintain slow and steady, stay under the radar, and don't make any waves. Then one day I woke up and found that we had ample working capital, credit, experience, goodwill, and credentials to step it up even further. I met others just like me who were taking bigger and bolder steps to set themselves up for exponential growth while making a huge impact in their communities. If they could do it, so could I. Years of experience have allowed me to set the company up for significant growth while maintaining what we can afford in regard to finances and time management.

Action Plan

The bottom line is, in order to grow at an exponential level, (which I define as two to four times your current size in five years), you should begin by contrasting how the public around you perceives you compared to your competition. A great way to place yourself on the good end of the contrast is to first determine which issues listed here might apply and then prioritize which ones you plan to solve and by when.

If you want to go big or go home, this list will help you begin the process of establishing big goals. I am happy to help you based on your setup, goals, and personality. I also developed a plan for you called "Advisor Transition Blueprint." If you want to download a copy for free, please go to https://advisortransitionblueprint.com/. Also contained on that site is our interview with Kevin Harrington.

I graduated from Tulane University with a BA in Economics and a minor in Computer Science in 1984. I started my career in technology development for the oil and gas industry. I helped to develop several companies, the most notable of which was Harmonic Systems, a collaboration of Exxon, MasterCard and Sprint. The company was sold to Alliance Data Systems in 2000. After successful projects including restaurants and my invention of CashPump, a bank ATM system intended to run at the gas pump, I began the design of a financial planning company in 2002, teamed up with Norman Strom in 2004, and Hunt and Strom Financial was born. In 2005, I learned about a highly rated stock and option trading platform called Thinkorswim (acquired by TD Ameritrade in January 2009) and integrated the solution into our financial practice. The purpose was to bring institutional quality money management to mass affluent clients at a reasonable price. Other advisors wanted the same for their clients, and that need created the formation of Redhawk Wealth Advisors, Inc. in 2008.

I reside in Tulsa, OK with my wife and two dogs. My two sons are grown and live in Colorado. I coached baseball and football for 12 years and served on the East Tonka Little League and Bennett Family Park boards. I also served 10 years as a Captain in the US Army and Reserves on the executive staff of the 486th Civil Affairs Company, 321st Special Operations Forces. I currently serve as a director on the Campbell-Lepley-Hunt Foundation Board of Directors, a charity organization that helps those in need all across the state of Oklahoma.

SCOTT KEFFER

The 3 Proven Methods to Make A Million in a Recession... And The ONE Sure-Fire Investment That Beats Them All

••••••••••••• TIPS •••••••••••••

1. Don't follow the crowd.
2. Invest in yourself.
3. Take one action today that gets you to your future self.

••••••••••••••••••••••••••••••••

My private clients want to know, "Scott, what should I do with my own money during a recession?"

When I heard, "There were more millionaires made in the Great Depression than any other time in U.S. history," I decided to look back at how they made their millions. I discovered 3 methods.

However, it still didn't compare with the ONE that beats them all.

To put it in perspective, $1 million dollars in 1930 is roughly equivalent to $15 million dollars at the writing of this book. According to data from the National Bureau of Economic Research, there have been 13 recessions since the Great Depression, which ended in 1933, which means there are more ahead.

Let's look at each of the three methods and the skills it takes to make a million.

Method 1: Investing

Many people lost fortunes, both big and small.

Black Tuesday. October 29, 1929. Billions were lost. Thousands were wiped out. Investors traded some 16 million shares on the New York Stock Exchange in a single day. Today, an average daily NYSE volume is around 1.2 million shares.

For the average investor, the road back was long. It took 25 years to recover from the Great Depression. It took 6 – 8 years to recover from the 2008 Great Recession.

Yet, some made millions through investing. Despite the Depression, new opportunities appeared for those with cash, a keen eye, guts... and patience.

When his father died in 1930, J. Paul Getty received a $500,000 inheritance and he took the helm as President of Getty Oil. Getty used the inheritance to buy oil stocks, at a discount, of course.

If you want to make a million in investments during a recession, you also need the ability to take risks. Be willing to speculate; to take action when others are paralyzed.

Method 2: Big Income

What's the one thing everyone wants in a recession (especially an extended recession)? Distractions; the more entertaining, the better.

During the Great Depression, most entertainers struggled like everyone else. However, a few became millionaires, like Gene Autry and Jimmy Cagney.

Autry, dubbed the "Singing Cowboy," was a local radio yodeler before the Depression. The 1930s were the start of hit song after hit song for him, which he leveraged into a movie career, eventually starring in over 90 movies. He would later create a radio and TV broadcasting empire, which allowed him to purchase the California Angels. Not bad for a local yodeler!

James Cagney, who had made a name in vaudeville, signed on as a contract movie actor, earning about $500 per week in 1930. By the mid-1930s, he was pulling in over $200,000 a year. Adjusted for inflation, that puts his income at over $3 million per year. Cagney would go on to star in 33 movies during the 1930s.

Method 3: Business

Many million-dollar fortunes were made by business owners. At least seven billion-dollar families owe their fortunes to young businesses that started during the Great Depression.

Michael Cullen quit his job in 1930 (I'm thinking his family and friends would not have been very supportive). Cullen had a stint as an executive at Kroger Grocery & Bakery Co., so he knew the challenges of bureaucracy. When his idea for a new kind of grocery store was rejected, he ventured out on his own. Within two years, his King Cullen Grocery stores were generating more than $6 million in sales—$90 million in today's numbers.

Howard Hughes released *Hell's Angels* at a cost of $3.8 million, a monstrous sum for a movie at that time. And, he released it AFTER the 1929 crash. In 1932, he launched the Hughes Aircraft Company, which would become a major supplier of defense equipment.

"We were brought up in the Depression. We weren't interested in the idea of making money. Our idea was: if you couldn't find a job, you'd make one for yourself." And, so they did. With $538, in a tiny garage in Palo Alto, California, Bill and Dave flipped a coin to determine whose name would appear first when identifying their new business. When Bill won the toss, Hewlett-Packard was born.

Charles Darrow lost his job in 1929. His idea took a few years to come to fruition, but he wasn't playing games.

Well, actually he was. Monopoly made him the first million-dollar game designer.

What does it take to make a million in business? Innovation.

There you have it. The 3 proven methods to make a million in a recession.

Investing. Speculation.

Big Income. Entertainment.

Business. Innovation.

Proven, yet only a very, very few make it using each method.

There is actually an investment that beats them all.

It works in a recession... or in an economic boon...

It is stunningly effective...

It has been proven over and over...

It is recommended by the successful...

And, it is available to all... regardless of your background or your current situation!

It is investing in yourself.

Henry Ford said, "Old men always advise the young to save money. This is bad advice. Invest in yourself."

After years of struggling with mediocre results, I remember reading this advice. I was skeptical. Then I heard it on a tape series. I wondered, "Will it work for me?"

I grew up shy and awkward and so I struggled with a poor picture of myself. It dawned on me that I wasn't willing to invest in myself because I was scared; scared to invest my money in me, because I felt like I was a loser.

I realized that by buying a book and a tape series, I *was* investing in myself. So, I decided to take the next step and invest in a coach. That's when things really began to change for me. Since then, I have invested over $1 million of my own money in coaching and training. It's been my best wealth-building investment. Hands down. Better than stocks, bonds, or any other investment.

Jim Rohn, a self-made multi-millionaire, business owner and author of over a dozen books on wealth and success said, "If you work on your job, you'll make a living. If you work on yourself, you'll make a fortune."

In the same vein, Dr. Stephen Covey, author of *The 7 Habits of Highly Successful People*, called it "sharpening the saw." He said, "Sharpening the saw means preserving and enhancing the greatest asset you have—you."

Here's Scott's Success Multiplier Formula.

> Dollars Invested in Personal Growth (DIPG)
> divided by
> Dollars Invested in Entertainment and Distraction (DIED)

What's your Success Multiplier Multiple?

Brian Tracy, legendary business trainer, bestselling author of over 70 books, and business consultant to over 1000 corporations said, "For every $1 you invest in yourself; it will return $30 to your bottom line."

30 to 1 ROI.

Want more money? More time? More energy?

Invest in yourself.

Here are three ways to invest in yourself.

Books

Jim Rohn was also famous for saying, "Poor people have big TVs. Rich people have big libraries."

Don't just read books, though. Make books happen.

As you read a book, highlight passages, and take notes. Also, use a square like this ☐ to indicate an action you could take. When you are finished, make a list of 3 actions you should take. Then, decide on ONE action you WILL take.

Charlie "Tremendous" Jones, author and editor of nine books, including *Life is Tremendous*, with over 2,000,000 in print, would often say, "You will be the same person in five years as you are today except for two things: the people you meet and the books you read."

Create a Top 10 Book List and make one book happen per month. In a year, YOU will be a different person.

⊃ If you'd like a copy of Scott's Must Have Personal Growth Books, email me at scott@ScottKeffer.com or go to ScottSharkBook.com.

When our children were teenagers, I would do an annual father/son outing with Joshua and father/daughter outing with Anni. We would go camping and hiking in Garrett State Park in Maryland. During one of our hikes through the woods at nearby Swallow Falls State Park, I encountered a sign which read: "In August 1918 and again in July 1921, Henry Ford, Thomas A. Edison, Harvey Firestone, John Burroughs and Company encamped here."

What were they doing together?

They were employing a success secret discovered and highlighted by Napoleon Hill in *Think and Grow Rich*. During many conversations with the highly successful businessman, Andrew Carnegie, Carnegie attributed his entire fortune and success to this one simple, yet powerful principle:

Mastermind Groups

Hill would say, "Analyze the record of any man who has accumulated a great fortune, and many of those who have accumulated modest fortunes, and you will find that they have either consciously or unconsciously employed the 'Master Mind' Principle."

Jim Rohn agreed and commented about the power of the mastermind principle, "You are the average of the five people you spend the most time with."

What Mastermind Group are you a committed member of?

To select one, I use the Running Faster Principle. If you want to run faster, run with people who are *already* running faster than you.

When I join a group, I employ the Give First Principle. First, give value. Going into a group, seek to add value first... and you will receive an abundance of value in return.

⮕ If you'd like a copy of Scott's Guide To Joining a Mastermind Group, email me at scott@ScottKeffer.com or go to ScottSharkBook.com.

Success leaves clues.

What did Apple's Steve Jobs, Google's Larry Page and Amazon's Jeff Bezos have in common with John D. Rockefeller? They all employed the same success secret:

Coaching

Jobs, Page and Bezos even shared the same coach, Bill Campbell, until he passed away. After his death, his impact on business leaders was highlighted in the book, *Trillion Dollar Coach*.

I almost quit investing in myself...

My commitment to invest in myself was severely tested when my wife, Beth, and I found ourselves in a half a million dollars of debt; $463,459.15 to be exact. Having made some poor business decisions, I had to exit my partner out of the business and take over all the business debt. It left us deep in the hole—economically and psychologically.

When the accountants reviewed our situation, they recommended that we immediately cut "two big expenses": marketing and coaching. It was a challenge. We were deep in debt.

Do we keep investing in marketing? No brainer! We wouldn't grow the business without marketing.

Do we keep investing in coaching? Then it dawned on me:

The business can't grow if I don't grow.

I told the bean-counters, "I will die quickly if I stop INVESTING (not spending) in coaching and training."

With God's grace and the coaching I continued to invest in, we were able to turn the company around and pay off all the business debt. Then we paid off all our personal debt. Then we built a multi-million-dollar business... and built our personal wealth.

Now we help others double, quadruple and 10x their business so that they can have the money, time and energy to make a BIG IMPACT® on their family, friends, clients and causes they care about deeply.

Isn't that cool? Now I get to pass it on!

Who's your coach? Harvey Mackay, business owner, *New York Times* bestselling author, and syndicated columnist agrees, "I have had twenty coaches, if you can believe it."

➲ If you'd like a copy of Scott's Top 10 Criteria For Hiring A Coach, email me at scott@ScottKeffer.com, go to ScottSharkBook.com, or call (412) 854-7860.

Jim Rohn put it best, "If you want to have more, you have to become more. For things to change, you have to change. For things to get better, you have to become better. If you improve, everything will improve for you. If you grow, your money will grow; your relationships, your health, your business and every external effect will mirror that growth in equal correlation."

Books. Mastermind Groups. Coaches.

Three proven methods to invest. Isn't it time YOU profit from the ONE sure-fire investment that pays off big time in a recession... or in an economic boon... or anytime.

YOU are your best investment.
Invest in yourself.
Start today!

Scott Keffer is an international Marketing and Business Growth Coach, Best Selling Author and Keynote Speaker, who you may have seen in or on NBC, CBS, FOX, PBS, CNBC, *Worth, Business Icons, Huffington Post, Wall Street Select, Research, Money Show, and Small Business Trendsetters,* among others. Keffer's seven books include: *Million Dollar Clients,* the #1 Amazon Best Seller *Double Your Affluent Clients* and *Million Dollar Clients With Seminars.* Keffer has spoken at most financial industry conferences, including The Forum 400, AALU, Ed Slott's Master Elite IRA Advisor Group, InsMark's Symposium, CRUMP, NFP, FIG, Advisors Excel, Global Wealth, Horter, BMO, National Network of Estate Planning Attorneys, Estate Planning Council, as well as a Visiting Scholar at High Point University. He has been hailed as an "industry transformer" as the Creator of many innovative processes, including Double Your Affluent Clients® Boot Camp, The Seminar Money Machine™, Million Dollar Clients Online™, The Donor Motivation Program®, The Affluent Engagement System®, and many others. Scott is the Founder and CEO of Scott Keffer International, where he and his team show financial advisors how to double their business by attracting Million Dollar E.L.K. Clients, so that they can take home more income, take off more time and have a BIG Impact® on their family, friends, clients and causes they care about deeply.

WILLIAM MCLAUGHLIN

Loss vs. Gain

Perception vs. Reality

"Even if you spend a lifetime saving and doing the right things, choosing the wrong investments and following the wrong advice just prior to or immediately after retirement can ruin everything"

Loss vs. Gain
Perception vs. Reality

When you sit down to plan your retirement, it's not uncommon to discover that what you have is not what you think you have.

So, what does that mean?

When we talk about risk exposure, most people don't really understand, or even know what their exposure to risk is. And we're not talking about stocks. Even moderate or conservative accounts, or "safe" investments that have a guarantee of principal, expose your portfolio to more risk than you might consider.

The risk of losing buying power due to inflation is often overlooked. There's the risk of conversion, resulting in what could be a great financial loss. This happens when certain instruments such as T-Bills are converted to income due to timing. I've heard that T-Bill conversion can be just as risky as the stock market. The possibility of a large disparity is possible when converting.

Often investors don't really know what types of mutual they are in to begin with, what kinds of redundancies they have, and what kinds of fees they are paying to the managers and brokers. Though the stock market is most commonly considered the epitome of risk with its volatility and unreliability, presumed safe accounts offer their own smorgasbord of risk with their lack of ability to produce income and keep pace with inflation. Think about it. You cannot have an abundant retirement if your money is peddling backwards.

Bob was a hardworking, professional turning sixty-five, wanting to make sure his "stuff" was in order; he sought out a second opinion. He was a disciplined saver and a do-it-your-selfer calling all the shots with his money and worked with a large reputable local bank, believing his money would be safe there. But like most people, he was concerned about running out of money during retirement.

Bob's father was in his late eighties and had just entered a nursing home. While helping his father and mother through this process he discovered just how much money it was going to require taking care of Dad. Bob was confident that he'd made safe choices for himself but wondered if he shouldn't be doing something more for himself to prepare for his own risks ahead. I'll never forget when Bob proclaimed at our initial visit that all his investments were safe.

"I have a conservative portfolio" he said proudly.

After just a very short period, I noticed that half of his money was in bank stock paying a little more than 1 percent, while the other half was in a brokerage account in similar funds doing exactly the same.

"May I pose a question?" I asked. "Which part of your portfolio is the safe part?"

If you invested in the last ten years, it's very likely that you have a mix of what is called "conservative" investments. The idea was that a portion of your savings into a growing position that would go up and down in value while a portion would be positioned to never decrease in value. The latter may have included Money market savings, cash alternatives, CD's, and bond funds. Unfortunately, in recent times these safe money alternatives have been getting low to zero return—which means one side of your portfolio has been earning nothing.

What's more, if there are any redundancies or overlap in your portfolio, this scenario—just another form of risk—is further negatively compounded. Bob was actually taking excessive risk in holding onto underperforming assets!

In short, the crux of a well-planned retirement can be summed up like this: stock market returns can be unreliable. CD's and other safe money returns may not be enough to keep up with inflation. Because no single investment is bulletproof today, retirees need more than one solution to keep their heads above water, stay in the game and ultimately retire abundantly.

The risk we talk about today is not just market risk, inflation, or taxes, risk can be complicated by the cost of growing old. As Bob found out the cost of nursing homes is rapidly rising faster than the current rate of inflation. Life expectancy figures from Social Security Administration show that men are living nineteen years longer than their parents, and women fifteen years longer. The Department of Health and Human Services says that most people turning sixty-five years old today will require some form of long-term care during their lives. (1) Co-pays, coinsurance, the escalating cost of assisted-living facilities and nursing homes can deplete savings in a matter of a few years or even months, depending on the level of care. It can't be emphasized strongly enough that anticipating those needs is one way to protect yourself from the risk of running out of money.

While still in our fifties and sixties it may be difficult to face the idea of physical or mental decline. Prolonged mortality is a mammoth challenge for everyone. It is said we are outliving our brains, bodies and wallets. Doctors and other medical professionals, health-care conglomerates, pharmaceutical companies, and hundreds of other entities are finding they need to step up to the plate in unanticipated ways to accommodate the phenomenon of a growing population of people in their eighties, nineties and centenarians—and those who are even older. In his book *Being Mortal,* Harvard Medical School professor and Brigham and Women's Hospital surgeon Atul Gawande says, "Modern scientific capability has profoundly altered the course of human life... We in the medical world have proved alarmingly unprepared for it" (2)

But what about you, the investor? Are you prepared?

It's easy to think that if you have a large 401(k) account balance, you're all set. But, are you?

Given the overwhelming statistics of our unpreparedness for long-term care, risk and longevity, it makes more sense to cast a wide net to address all the issues that could cut into your peace of mind while entertaining an abundant retirement. Having a growth component to your retirement plan is crucial.

So, what can you use to augment your retirement savings and prepare for what may be inevitable?

Today's retirees have access to tools that address the issue of long-term care. In the past, traditional (expensive) long-term care insurance was the only alternative. Use it or lose it proposition, if not used you forfeited all the premiums paid.

Today there are many life insurance tools that exist that put a tax-free asset on the books that either you will use for your care or you will leave as a legacy to your beneficiaries.

Depending on you wants and desires, your advisor should explore the large array of tools and options and let you know what is available to you that will serve you best. By the same token, it is advised to use a specialist that will serve you all of your days.

While my Mom was an athlete and very outgoing, my Dad on the other hand was a chemical engineer—cerebral and introverted. He had an IQ that was off the charts, he didn't say a lot and as I found out had no clue about what to do with his money.

I grew up one of six kids in a middle-class neighborhood in South Jersey. Dad and I were never really very close. I was pretty sure he didn't even know what I did for a living, until one day, when he was sixty-three, I got a call out of the blue asking if I was a broker.

Ouch! "No Dad", I told him, "I am a Certified Financial Planner and specialize in retirement."

"Yeah, Yeah, Yeah" he said, "So you deal with money?"

My dad and I never talked about money in our entire lives and he'd spent his life working in corporate America. Now he was facing retirement.

Mobil Oil had offered him a retirement package, and he wanted to know what to do. What were his options? Should he retire and take the lump-sum pension? Should he move his 401(k)? And what about Social Security?

Even if you spend a lifetime saving and doing the right things, choosing the wrong investments and following the wrong advice just prior to and immediately following retirement can ruin everything. It can prove detrimental to the longevity your retirement income. As a retiree responsible for the growth and maintenance of your savings, and anything else that comes along, as it did with my Dad, following unhelpful advice from a well-meaning but poorly trained broker often happens because you don't know any better.

As you transition from accumulation to distribution years, growth and income needs change. It can be uncomfortable to acknowledge that the individual that got you here can't help you going forward. You have outgrown him or her and are likely not the right one to get you through your retirement.

So, what's the difference between a broke/advisor or a specialist/advisor?

First, building a successful retirement takes three things: time, money and change.

Many people get the money part right, and during retirement, you have a lot of time. But having to change usually presents a problem. People are creatures of habit, finding it difficult to change the way they've been doing things and with whom they've been doing them with. In fact, the older we get the harder it is to change.

The choices are simple when choosing a financial partner. A broker, whose job is to work with everyone or a specialist who only works with likeminded retirees, a broker, whose standard, is "suitable" or a fiduciary, whose legally liable and required to by law to consider investments that are in your best interest?

Take a moment to consider your future in retirement. What do you want it to look like? Are you meeting your own needs? Are you happy with the way things are working out now? What do you really want when it comes to your lifestyle and your legacy?

Are you prepared to finish strong?

1. U.S. Department of Health and Human Services, "Find your path forward: The Basics," Long Term Care.gov, https://longtermcare.acl.gov/the-basics/.

2. Atul Gawande, Being Mortal, (Metropolitan Books, Henry Holt and Company. 2014), 6.

William "Bill" J. McLaughlin, CFP®, CLU®, ChFC®, is a nationally recognized financial educator, author, speaker and retirement planner, whom you may have seen on NBC, ABC, CBS, and Fox network affiliates, or in *Yahoo News, Wall Street Journal's Market Watch, Wall Street Select, New York Business Journal,* and others.

Bill is a contributing author of *Retire Abundantly*. As the founder of McLaughlin Financial Group, Bill and his team show retired business owners, professionals, and women on their own how to more fully preserve, protect and pass on their hard-earned money. Bill and his wife live in Wall, New Jersey, where they enjoy the natural beauty of the Jersey coastline.

JAMES T. NIEMEYER

Does Gratitude Matter?

"Do anything, but let it produce joy!"
—Walt Whitman, Poet

••••••••••••• **TIPS** ••••••••••••••

1. Always engage a collaborative team of advisors so that advice is not given in silos.

2. Always convey to at least one advisor a complete set of objectives and time frame for completion and have that advisor share those objectives with all the other advisors.

3. Always "think with the end in mind!" That is, if all a client's objectives were to be fulfilled what would it look like? Strategy before Tactics is the Golden Rule.

••••••••••••••••••••••••••••••••

"It was the best of times and the worst of times" (Charles Dickens). Does this sound like your business, or perhaps your life?

Each of us, while we pursue our respective life's calling, creates our own reality whether we realize it or not. We work in concert and collaboration with others and perhaps, without even knowing, our vibrational selves. We each have both a physical and a vibrational self. Some would label the vibrational self the soul, inner guidance, a guardian angel, source, or perhaps a conscience. It's the feeling that we're either on the right path or that something unwanted is entering our lives.

Life brings contrasts. That is, life brings each of us moment to moment glimpses of both what we want and what we don't want. The major challenge in life is sifting through the myriad of choices while maintaining focus on what it is that we really want. The critical element in maintaining a state of consciousness that allows us to create what we really want into our lives is Gratitude.

Ask and it is given is a basic tenant of all the world's wisdom traditions. But asking from a state of thankfulness, grace and love tends to lessen resistance and increase allowance.

But what about my goals and life objectives for my business and my family you ask? Won't I have to work hard and sacrifice? Won't there be substantial pain and suffering in order to fulfill those objectives and realize the rewards of wealth, abundance, love, and security. The answers seem self-evident since that's the dominant culture in which we live. In other words, we've bought into the groupthink that these are the only ways to "succeed" in life.

Work hard. Sacrifice for your family. Give up current pleasure for future rewards. And while you're doing all of that are you experiencing joy? Are you feeling that it's all worth it? When a certain goal is accomplished isn't there another and another goal or objective? And doesn't the cycle begin all over again with seemingly no end in sight?

Stop! And what I mean by that is to, at any given moment and all given moments, stop. Stop and give thanks and express gratitude for both what you've accomplished and for the contrast, or the challenges that seem endless. Soften your resolve rather than continuing to struggle. Struggle tends to create more struggles since what we think about, we bring about.

Notice the negative aspects of your creation, own them and claim responsibility for them and then...give thanks and express extreme gratitude for those negative aspects that lead you to define what it is that you really want. Another aspect of claiming responsibility is assessing the risks associated with one's business or family. Sound planning includes appropriate trusts, wills, healthcare directives and assessing and insuring the "Elements of Fate" in one's life. Those are Business Risk, Market Risk and Mortality and Morbidity Risk. Be grateful that our economic system has evolved to the point where we can adequately assess and address those elements.

And then, after you've noticed what you don't want and defined what you do want, let it go and trust that the basic tenant of the world's wisdom tradition is true. Ask and it is given doesn't mean bitch and complain about what you don't have. It means that for which you've asked has ALREADY been given. And the only way to access what's already been given is to express joy and gratitude for the journey and unfolding.

But, but, but I don't see it yet so how could it be given? We've been taught to say, "I'll believe it when I see it." However, that's not really how the universe works. A preferred course of action is simply allowing it into your consciousness when it's ready to manifest. In words, I'll see it WHEN I believe it.

We all struggle with doubt. Sometimes we move to hope and often to belief. Note the progression of doubt, hope and belief. The destination is "knowing". That is, one positively knows that the laws of the universe are working for our benefit. Your inner being, your soul, your vibrational self knows it. If you quiet your mind and listen, you'll hear it. If you close your eyes you will see. If you quiet your thoughts you will feel that your soul, your vibrational self is ALWAYs there for you with love and support.

There's NEVER a disconnection from your Source, or inner being. The critical element is following the path of least resistance which is also the path of most allowance. Life is meant to be a never-ending, joyous journey and practicality will kill the momentum.

We all walk around most of time oblivious to our inner guidance. We are all so free that we are so free that we can chose bondage. And by buying to the groupthink we miss out on the joy of continuous creation and unfolding while on the journey. Words rarely teach. Only life experiences teach.

Refrain from responding to life conditionally. That is, for example, I'll only be happy when I make the next sale. I'll only be happy when I have the new car. I'll only be happy if my friends or lover act or accept me in a certain way. Moment to moment recognize that there is NOTHING more valuable in life than the joy of being connected to who you really are. It catalyzes new, moment to moment experiences and "ah ahs."

Nothing will keep you from your connection with your inner guidance or source more than feeling bad. So, listen to that music that uplifts you. Read that passage that inspires you. Look at your family and feel the joy and inspiration that you and your companions have joined you in the cocreation of your life.

Reach moment to moment for the feelings of joy; for those feelings of unconditional love. For it is your feelings that will guide you to that which you seek. After all, "ask and it is given" means just that. It's already given in escrow and is available to you only when you bring yourself into alignment with inner being or vibrational self. You'll know it when you "feel" it. It's the only way to see the money in your bank account, the lover in your life and the fulfillment of your purpose. Connecting moment to moment with all that you want in your life is to acknowledge and connect with your inner being. With your source. With your soul.

And the way to access all that is already given. The way to bring into physical reality all that is awaiting you in escrow, that way to have the love of your life, the wonderful successful business, the money in your bank account is to live a life of GRATITUDE.

You've moved from doubt to hope to belief. Now, isn't it time to KNOW how full your life is by simply acknowledging your gratitude for ALL that has been given. Notice that there's a distinct difference between thinking thoughts and receiving thoughts. Turn, moment to moment, to what feels good. Refrain from being a conditional responder to life. That is, "I will only feel good if...." You have not been born into this physical reality to suffer. You're here to recognize your life's purpose and joyfully fulfill it.

And when you are enjoying the journey, moment to moment, day to day, you'll realize I've truly figured out my relationship with me and I'm constantly aware of my vibrational relationship with who I really am and what I really want. I guide every thought I can to mesh with the wholeness that I am, and I've become a deliberate thinker and I no longer create by default. I think on purpose, I speak on purpose, and I act on purpose and don't do any of these unless I'm connected to who I really am. That connection can always be accessed while in a state of gratitude and love. As a matter of fact, it can only be accessed in a state of gratitude and love.

Does gratitude matter? Well, you'll have to meditate upon that question. Perhaps even for the next moment, then the next hour, the next day, or even for the rest of your life. For once you acknowledge that that's your connection with your true self, you'll realize that gratitude and love are not just empty platitudes. They are the keys to the kingdom. For truly, it all lies within you. All that you've asked for is already there. It's your responsibility to own it and bring it into your physical reality. And know you truly know how to "Build Wealth like a Shark." Be grateful.

Acknowledgement: With extreme gratitude to Jo, Esther and Jerry Hicks, Abraham Andyes, my own connection with the Source within.

Jim T. Niemeyer has 50+ years as a financial services practitioner. He has established and funded Supplemental Executive Retirement Plans (SERPs) for public corporations. Jim has collaborated in the development of income and estate tax mitigation strategies as well as charitable giving strategies. He works only in collaboration with top ranked legal, wealth management and accounting advisors in the Western United States. His hobbies are sailing, skiing, mountain biking, golfing, self-examination and improvement. He's a diligent and thorough practitioner who first establishes client objectives and brings together only the most qualified practitioners to collaborate in fulfillment of client goals. The quality of the questions he asks are the "power tools" of innovation and solution.

ANTHONY ROBERTS

Procrastination

·············· TIPS ··············

1. Start your Financial Planning Preparation Today!
2. Work with Professionals who utilize all Financial Planning Tools on your behalf.
3. Make sure when working with a Professional they know your vision and desires.

·································

Procrastination, the excuse to wait.

But why? I think it was Mark Twain who said in twenty years we will regret more the things we did not attempt to do than those things accomplished. Also, you've probably heard the ancient Chinese proverb which said the best time to plant a tree is fifty years ago and the second-best time is today.

There appear to be three main factors affecting our reasoning to delay our planning for retirement.

The first revolves around the "pain" avoidance. Whether it be lack of money, lack of time or lack of confidence, if we never face the current situation or the future scenario then we will always maintain a 50-50-coin flip philosophy confirming I'm good or bad.

According to a study conducted in 2018 by *Fidelity Investments,* seventy-five percent of us put off planning for the future and the top activities avoided are:

- Creating a Budget—30%
- Creating/Updating Estate Plan/Will—30%
- Setting up an Emergency Fund—27%
- Paying down Debt—26%
- Saving for Retirement—25%

If you never go to the doctor, then you will never have the pain of the shot or the bad news from the test results. Many people just find it more comforting to live each day as it is and not worry about tomorrow. What they may be saying is, "I do not want the consequences of knowing what tomorrow may bring."

This brings us to the second reason for avoidance which quite simply is refusing to make or prepare a proper plan. The financial industry has created a myth which states as long as you work tirelessly, contribute the maximum amount sustainable to your retirement plans and agree to pull out no more than four percent per year during retirement, you **SHOULD** be okay. Unfortunately, the 2008 years came along and now our portfolio is down 40% and the four percent withdrawal now needs to be seven percent to make up the difference and so on and so on. Downward spiral, not good.

Question, if I were to ask you one week after the 2008 financial crisis if having a chance to do over, would you continue to have your investments aligned the same or would you have made changes? There is no right or wrong answer to this question but there are right and wrong consequences. Once retired, for the most part you lose the "Do Over" option. During our twenties, thirties and forties we have a key factor on our side which allows us to sustain and overcome. It's called time. However, once retired we may still have thirty-five years of life to live but if retired, we have no outside income. Thus, the significance of getting it right and having a structured plan which is stress tested to survive the bad as well as the good times.

Withdrawing 4% and receiving monthly account statements is not a plan.

Another myth which surfaces regularly with proper financial planning involves what financial instruments to use to manufacture liquidity and maintain wealth. Investments such as stocks, bonds and ETF's have their place within a well-rounded portfolio but there also can be uses for such tools as fixed indexed annuities and life insurance.

There are hundreds of companies offering thousands upon thousands of these financial investments. How do you determine if one is better than the other or if investing in multiple strategies reduces your risk while still allowing growth? These are just some of the questions you should be having with your advisor so you can determine what path is right for you.

Notice using ALL financial instruments may be beneficial to you. Unfortunately, there exist professionals who believe 100% of the time the plans need to be designed through the same template for all utilizing the same investment strategies. Some people need to be wholly invested in managed money accounts while others may need to be all in with annuities and life insurance. Reality is, with most cases, the client needs to be diversified across all avenues for maximum liquidity, growth and protection.

Make sure your advisor has the ability to use all the tools in his or her financial tool chest for your benefit and planning.

The third avoidance reason is one of being overwhelmed. We live in a day of DIY (Do It Yourself) and quite frankly, we cannot always do what we don't know.

I once had a very successful plastic molding business owner attend one of our retirement and tax planning workshops. At the end of the workshop he let me know he took care of all of his planning work. Maybe I was being a bit coy, but I told him over the past weekend I had spent time downloading how to be a plastic mold technician and I just wondered if he would give me a job. As you might guess, his response was of course not. I proceeded to ask him how many of the approximate 104 estate and tax planning strategies he had incorporated into his own plan. The look was one of confusion and doubt.

I tell the above story not to cast a bad light on the gentleman but to bring notice to the fact, that if we don't

Procrastination

know the questions to ask, then how can we possibly expect to achieve a correct answer? The issue is not trying to be as versed as possible but understanding there are professional advisors who have spent their lifetime sharpening their craft in order to lend their knowledge to the betterment of their clients.

In addition to the overwhelming sensation, many times people, when dealing with current or future financial responsibilities, will begin to overstress or even go to the point of feeling ashamed. The older one gets, multiplied by the feeling they have not been successful enough, tends to cloud one's thinking. Saying there's not enough there, then why bother or deciding there's no use to start because catching up can never happen, are additional components of the procrastination event.

Quit beating yourself up but accept responsibility and accountability to improve your situation or to achieve that next, higher step. Only you control the person viewing you in the mirror each morning. I know in my down times I was picked up by a friend quoting an unknown source stating the following:

"Failure is not being knocked down but the refusal to get back up!"

We've all come up short and yes, we have all failed, however by continuing to push forward the dark becomes light and the vision starts to become clear in producing the clarity for accomplishing desired goals.

The desire to move forward should be outlined as follows:

1. Begin
   a. There has never been an "end" achieved without a beginning. Quit waiting, quit procrastinating, quit making excuses and desire to move forward. Know waiting for 100% of the questions to be answered will never exist. The best you can hope for is to gather as much information as possible and to surround yourself with as much expertise as possible in order to make the soundest decisions possible. You may even make a few bad decisions but that's okay. A bad decision is sometimes better than no decision at all.
2. Surround yourself with a proven professional
   a. John Rockefeller once said, and this is paraphrased.... Things I can do well, I'll do myself but those things I cannot do well, I will seek out the help of others and pay them to do so. If one of the most successful businessmen in the history of our country could understand his short-comings and seek assistance, then doesn't that possibly make sense for you?
   b. Have you ever wondered why there are not more multi-sport superstars? Other than possibly Bo Jackson, I cannot recall any sports legend who has been able to compete at the highest level in multiple sports. You may say Deion Sanders or Michael Jordan played two professional sports, but it was fairly evident they didn't master their second

sport. Why do you think this occurs? Possibly because it is so very difficult to master one profession, and there exists not the time nor energy to devote to the second sport.
   i. The same exists with choosing the proper professional to assist you. In all likelihood you are going to miss something if you try to do it on your own, whereas a dedicated professional can select strategies and designs to complement your personality and planning visions.
  c. Having proven professionals surrounding you in multi areas such as finance, accounting, legal and business are essential tools.

3. Do what you want
  a. Many times, the professional forgets one very important component, do they know your vision and desires. It is very important for your vision to define clarity in order to achieve your goals. One of the biggest mistakes I see advisors make is lending their pre-conceived notions to what they think you want. Basically, they are not asking the right questions and more importantly, they are failing to do proper listening.
   i. Remember
      1. Vision
      2. Clarity
      3. Goals

4. Have a "blueprint" prepared
   a. I remember growing up and taking a trip, we'd head down to the AAA office and a "Trip Tic" was provided. It basically said you started here and ended up there with the flip maps in between for direction. Now we call that Google Maps! Regardless, you cannot act on a plan if at first you don't design one. Builders and sub-contractors have to have an architect provide the design in order for them to build the house.
      i. The same is true for your financial plan, contract with an advisor who can develop the design in order for the plan to be carried out.
      ii. Also remember, many times the advisor who designs the plan can also carry out the investment details, whether they be managed assets or fixed insurance products. Either way, if you allow one firm to represent being the "architect, builder and sub-contractors", it usually results in fee reductions for you.
5. Just Do It
   a. A shoe company has made a fortune out of that command. The command doesn't say think about and perhaps act later. It says, "DO IT!"

Develop a deadline to start accomplishing the tasks above and from there, do not look back. Anyone who has accomplished a task has always felt better and more at ease knowing there was work to be done and now it's been completed.

To close, I'll mention Einstein's 8th wonder of the world…. Compound. Many of us believe the compound effect results in build-up and multiples, however, the compound effect can act as just a severe negative when one allows the compounding of in-action to accumulate as well.

Good luck, GOD Bless, and may your vision define your dreams!

ANTHONY "TONY" S. ROBERTS, CHFC®, CSA is a nationally recognized Financial Educator, Author, Speaker and Retirement Planner, whom you may have seen on or in *NBC, ABC, CBS,* and *FOX network affiliates* and *Bloomberg Business, Yahoo Finance, Investing Daily, Wall Street Select, Market Watch, The Louisville Courier Journal, Louisville TOPS magazine* and others. As the Creator of The Abundant Wealth Process™ and Founder of Prosperity Asset Management, LLC, Tony and his team have been helping business owners, professionals and executives preserve, protect and pass on their wealth for over 30 years.

MARK SHERWIN

The 1 Thing You Need to Know About Money

"Rule No. 1 is never lose money. Rule No. 2 is never forget Rule No. 1."
—Warren Buffet

Do you remember the hit comedy City Slickers? This comedy from the early 90's shared the vision, insight, and wisdom of a cowboy played by Jack Palance with the City Slickers lead by comedian Billy Crystal. While on western cattle drive Curly, played by Jack Palance, and Mitch, played by Billy Crystal, left the group to search for stray cattle. Curly asked Mitch, "Do you know the secret of life?" Mitch says, "No, what?" Curly holds up one finger. Mitch says, "Your finger?" Curly says, "One thing. Just one thing; stick to it, and everything else doesn't mean sh*t." Mitch says, "That's great, but what's the one thing?" Curly says, "That's what you need to figure out." A character in a hit comedy was able to share the secret to success.

Simply do the most important thing to get what you want. It's very simple. Ignore all the things you could do and simply do the one thing you should do.

Gary Keller, author of "The One Thing," shared a focusing question with readers that asks:

> **"What's the one thing I can do such that by doing it everything else will be easier or unnecessary?"**

We have adapted that question to "What is the one thing I can do that will secure my family's financial future, goals, and aspirations?" We start with aspirations, but for the purposes of this chapter, we will focus on the one thing we must "Do Now" to secure our financial future.

So, we must ask ourselves what is the major danger to our financial security? What's the one thing? Well, I like to look to the experts, and Warren Buffet lives by a rule regarding wealth and financial security.

Warren Buffett states:
**"Rule #1 Never Lose Money.
Rule # 2 Never Forget Rule # 1**

Then we ask, "What is the major danger to financial security, and how do we make it, so we never lose money?"

We believe the major danger to financial security is taxes.

So, let's ask ourselves, "What one thing can I do now to mitigate and eliminate future taxation, and by doing it, everything else will be easier or unnecessary?"

You see, the issue of tax is a modern-day strategic dilemma. A modern-day strategic dilemma is something that is:

1. Unsolvable

2. Recurrent
3. Complex
4. Threatening

As of June 2019, U.S. Debt was $22 Trillion. That amounts to $181,646 per taxpayer. *(U.S. Debt Clock)*

But that is not the true debt. That's only this current year's debt.

Future unfunded liabilities, including Social Security and Medicare, are $122 Trillion. That's $1,010,617 per taxpayer. *(U.S. Debt Clock)*

So, taxes will have to go up! That is a modern-day strategic dilemma.

John Maynard Keynes wisely states:

"The avoidance of taxes is the only intellectual pursuit that still carries any reward."

So, what's the one thing I can do to mitigate and eliminate future taxation? We are told by the mass media and financial institutions that deferring taxes is the first thing to do in tax and retirement planning. The mass media and financial institutions then recommend IRAs, 401(k)s, SEPs, 403(b)s, TSPs, and other such vehicles to defer current year taxation.

However, there are many limits, controls, and possible penalties in traditional IRAs, 401(k)s and the like:

1. IRA contribution limits are $6,000 for people under age 50 and $7,000 for people over age 50.
2. 401(k) contribution limits for someone under 50 is $19,000 and $25,000 for someone over 50.
3. Contributions are tax-deferred, so income tax is owed on any withdrawal during retirement.
4. There is a 10% penalty for accessing your hard earned funds prior to age 59 ½.
5. If you don't want or need to access your funds in retirement, the government will force withdrawals after you are 70 ½. These are called Required Minimum Distributions.

So, the government puts tight limits on how much we are able to contribute and enforces severe penalties if we need to access our money before retiring. Basically, these are known as age and use restrictions.

There is a Mortgage on Your Hard-Earned Money

Because you received an up-front tax deduction on the contribution to your IRA and 401(k), you will owe taxes when you access your hard-earned retirement savings. So that IRA or 401(k) balance is not real money. Much of that balance will be lost to income tax when you withdraw your funds. It's akin to a mortgage on your house. Your house has a market value, but if you sold it and still had a mortgage, you would only receive the difference between the amount your home sold for and the mortgage balance. It's similar with your IRA and 401(k). Instead of the mortgage, you will owe taxes on any withdrawal.

And you will be taxed at your highest income tax rate at both the federal and state levels. Accessing those funds could also move you into the next higher tax bracket. You will be taxed when you withdraw those retirement funds for living expenses, travel, healthcare, and more. You will be taxed at your highest rate even though you no longer work or earn an income.

Even if you don't need all of your money during retirement and want to pass your tax-deferred funds to your children, you will be forced to take Required Minimum Distributions the year after you turn 70½. That money will be taxed and anything left for your children will then be taxed at your children's highest income tax bracket and could even push them into a higher tax bracket.

You Have a Choice between Tax-Deferred and Tax-Free

Instead of the traditional IRAs and 401(k), you can make contributions to tax-free vehicles such as the Roth IRA and 401(k) and I strongly suggest that my clients consider the Roth. There are, however, many restrictions that limit our ability to take advantage of the Roth.

- There are income limits.
    - If you make too much money, the government won't allow you to participate

- There are contribution limits.
  - The same limits in the traditional IRA and 401(k) apply.

The advantage of the Roth is that you pay income tax prior to making the contribution so the dollars will grow tax-deferred and you will have access to income tax free assuming certain time frames are met. The dollars you access in retirement will be income tax-free so you will be able to spend the same amount of dollars you withdraw. This is extremely important in the distribution phase of your life.

The second option of tax-free investing is municipal bonds, but most clients don't believe municipal bonds are a good fit in today's low yield environment.

The third option for allocation of dollars into tax-free vehicles is cash value life insurance that utilizes section 7702 of the Internal Revenue Code. Many clients utilize cash value life insurance for one reason. The limits imposed by the government on IRA's, 401(k)'s and Roth's don't apply.

There are:
- No income limits
- No contribution limits
- No 10% penalty for accessing funds prior to 59 ½
- Your cash value is 100% principal protected from stock market losses

This is Not Your Dad's Insurance

Most people aren't excited to talk about insurance, and we agree. When most people think of insurance, they are thinking of home insurance, auto insurance, and health insurance. Insurance is thought of as an expense or a necessary evil. When thinking about life insurance, they are thinking about term insurance that will only benefit their family when the insured dies. Although we love our families and want the best for them, it can be difficult for consideration of life insurance to get to the top of the list of priorities. We don't get excited about those old forms of insurance either!

Traditional insurance has been about indemnification of loss when something bad happens. Now, there is a basic shift underway in the insurance industry from insuring purely against loss to a focus on risk and risk transfer. There are now risks we may choose to eliminate or transfer risk away beyond what is considered traditional or "old school" insurance.

We encourage our clients to consider cash value life insurance utilizing section 7702 of the Internal Revenue Code and these plans have been around for over 100 years. Today, there are a handful of 7702 plans that offer modern-day upgrades to help overcome modern-day strategic dilemmas.

The Modern-day 7702 plans are a superb example of the insurance industry moving from purely traditional "old school" indemnification to a modern day focus on risk transfer while also insuring against loss.

Modern-day 7702 plan benefits include:

1. Increased cash value when stock market indices go up
2. No loss due to stock market indices loss
3. Grows tax-deferred
4. Allows tax-free access
5. No pre-59½ penalty for access
6. Is low cost

This strategy helps combat the modern-day strategic dilemma of government spending, which leads to continued and likely increased taxation. When section 7702 is followed, it allows for the benefits we listed above, such as tax-deferred growth, tax-free access, and more.

In fact, Ed Slott CPA, the preeminent authority on IRAs says,

"The Tax Exemption for Life Insurance is the Single Biggest Benefit in the Tax Code. Period."

With your modern-day 7702 plan, there is no mortgage. You have successfully gotten your dollars off the future tax grid. The balance is yours to spend!

What to do next...

If you have found the information in this chapter to be of value and you would like to learn more, simply visit my website.

To receive a Free Report about America's Retirement Crisis, go to:
www.ourretirementcrisis.com

To learn more about Lifestyle & Legacy Protection go to:
www.lifestyleandlegacyprotection.com

To schedule a 1 on 1 conversation about The Lifestyle & Legacy Protection Process, you can email Mark Sherwin at msherwin@llprotection.com or call 813 490 9126.

Mark Sherwin has been in the financial industry for over 25 years; and, in 2001 founded Sage Capital Advisors, Inc. now called Sage Capital Concepts, Inc. Mr. Sherwin attended the University of Florida, Eckerd College, and Albert Ludwig's Universität earning both a B.A. in International Business and a B.A. in German. He has held the Series 7, Series 24 and Series 65 as well as the 214 licenses.

Mr. Sherwin is a provider of continuing education to CPAs and attorneys practicing in Florida regarding Lifestyle & Legacy Protection.

Mr. Sherwin, an accomplished author and speaker, has given lectures on advanced business and estate planning strategies at:

- Florida Symposium of the Financial Planning Association
- Tampa Financial Planning Association
- Tampa Society of Financial Service Professionals
- Numerous Private Law and Accounting Firms

Mr. Sherwin is a Fox Business News Contributor and has been featured on TanTalk Radio Network, 1250 WHNZ Impact Radio and CBS Radio Tampa Bay.

ART SOBCZAK

The Sandbox Doesn't Have to Be a Dirty Place

"The way a team plays as a whole determines its success. You may have the greatest bunch of individual stars in the world, but if they don't play together, the club won't be worth a dime."
—Babe Ruth

••••••••••••••• TIPS ••••••••••••••

1. Take charge of your sandbox
2. Hire advisors who share the sandbox
3. Add some special sand for special structures

••••••••••••••••••••••••••••••••

The Sandbox Doesn't Have to Be a Dirty Place
The young man of 28 stood triumphantly at the head of the conference table as the meeting ended. He was smiling and shaking hands with his new client, Harry. He had just

been hired to lead Harry's advisory team in developing a comprehensive plan for his business and family objectives. The other members of the advisory team were filing out quickly. They seemed focused on getting out of the room. Perhaps they had busy schedules and didn't have time for post meeting chit chat. That was fine with the young man. He didn't really need them anyway. This was his sandbox now...

It's 1988 and 48-year-old Harry's Midwest manufacturing company is profitable. Prospects are looking good for continued growth and prosperity. He has a loving wife and two kids in their 20's, both recent college graduates. One had just started at the company and the other was off to a career in nursing. Harry liked this confident, well dressed and polished young fella. He was a breath of fresh air, enthusiastic and engaging. He wasn't shy about addressing questions throughout his dynamic and organized presentation. He had answers to Harry's legal questions. He had answers to accounting questions. He had answers to investing questions. He masterfully addressed any concern in such a way that his CPA, attorney and investment advisor, all of whom were at the meeting, must have been impressed with his broad knowledge and keen abilities. Harry patted the young life insurance agent on the back and told him he was looking forward to getting started.

As the other advisors were moving swiftly from the room, one held back until Harry and the others had left. It was the CPA. He was clearly well-heeled and had been seated closely to Harry. He approached the young man, put his arm around him and asked, "Would you mind if I staked you a little professional advice?"

Our intrepid young insurance agent didn't feel the need for any advice from the likes of an accountant. After all, he'd been taught formally and informally in his vast five years of experience, that the other advisors were of no consequence. Inviting them to a final proposal meeting was a professional courtesy. He knew that they wouldn't recognize a creative idea if it sat down to dinner with them. He was trained to recognize that CPAs are historians. They look in the rear-view mirror and tell a client what happened to their finances and how to report it. Attorneys on the other hand are deal-killers and document-writers. He knew their job is to memorialize in writing the details of business transactions and to make business and personal agreements that support the planning objectives identified and implemented by folks like himself. Investment advisors? They're commission whores looking for the next transaction with a goal of accumulating and controlling a client's investable assets. Life Insurance agents, by nature of their need to think many years into the future, to a client's death and beyond, are perfectly suited to be the central planning partner for successful clients. It's self-evident and everyone knows that, right?

With a smug smile and an air of confidence the agent answered, "Sure, what's up?" Gently, the CPA started, "Young man, didn't your mother ever tell you to play nice in the sandbox?" He motioned to the agent to have a seat and continued, "First, I must say you certainly are good.

You're polished, persuasive and you engender a certain confidence I could only wish upon my junior associates. That said, you treated the rest of us as though we were invisible. It's like you came into the sandbox with your bucket and took over. You dug holes, made piles and didn't ask if anyone else wanted to help with whatever it was you were doing. At first it looked like it could be fun. It seemed you knew what you wanted to do. However, you just kept expanding the dig and making bigger piles. The rest of us were forced to play along the edges of the box. That was no fun, and as you saw, after the meeting everyone else picked up their proverbial toys and went home." The CPA sat back in his chair and let the young agent reflect for a moment, then asked, "Would it be safe to assume that the other advisors in the room have more clients like Harry?" The agent nodded in affirmation. "And after today, do you think any of us will invite you to play in the sandbox with our other clients?" he asked. He continued, "You rode roughshod over our comments, you dismissed our presence as an annoyance, you addressed every question as though you are the fountain of all knowledge. You didn't give any of us the professional courtesy to address Harry's questions that fell within the purview of our expertise. As a result, it may not be easy to work with us as you develop YOUR plans for Harry. Whether it's copies of investment statements, tax returns or legal documents, your information requests might not make it to the tops of our action piles. Do you think that might have an impact on the accuracy and validity of your work?"

When the CPA had finished, he sat back in his conference chair and stared intently at the young man. Normally he wouldn't have invested his time, wisdom and energy into an insurance agent, but something told him to take a chance on this one. Clearly this young man was thinking, not reacting. After what seemed like an eternity, the agent leaned forward with a look of resolve and contrition and said, "I'm sorry. Everything you've said is absolutely right. My business would be a lot easier and more fun if I could partner with other advisors. How could I have been so blind?" he exclaimed. "It's not your fault," the CPA said reassuringly. "It's the way you were taught, but not the way things really are. How about you come to my office tomorrow afternoon, say around three o'clock? If you're open to some mentoring, we can start a journey to transform your career from lone wolf life insurance agent, to collaborative professional colleague. It's your choice." Standing, I shook his hand and said, "I'm grateful. See you tomorrow."

And so the journey began. I learned a lot that next morning, and over the next three decades. Working alongside financial advisors, money managers, CPAs, attorneys, and family office executives, I learned that attorneys are not deal-killers. Wonder of wonders! They are bright, intelligent and often creative professionals who have a passion for protecting their clients through masterfully crafted documentation. I learned that most CPAs are more than rear-view mirror tacticians. They too are bright, intelligent and extremely knowledgeable about looking to the future to help business owners enhance the value of their companies. Often they are the client's most trusted advisor. Financial advisors know a heck of a lot about strategies and tactics that not only build financial wealth, but do so with an eye on tax management. Their services and skills are compensated fairly, and the vast majority are honest, helpful and hardworking. And while most of them have an insurance license, the ones working with affluent clients would rather bring a tried and true specialist to the relationship when the client's objectives far surpass the need for what I call level one income protection planning.

In the end, it is the client who decides who gets on the advisory team and who doesn't. Unfortunately, the advisors they "grew up with" aren't always the ones to take them to the next level of planning. Sometimes a specialist is needed.

Let me tell you about Frank, for example. We worked with Frank and his team on some advanced planning techniques that included the addition of significant life insurance premium commitments. Frank has been paying hundreds of thousands in taxes due to his high income from his business and invested assets. In reviewing his documents, we could see the complexity of his taxable situation. Now this was the hard part. I knew of a specialty CPA firm that reviews tax returns for clients with personal taxable incomes in excess of $1 million, and who own a business or have other complex holdings. Their deal is this; if they can find some tax refunds using their expanded universe of tools and techniques just for these sorts of clients, they get a percentage of the savings as a fee. If they don't find any ways to help, there is no charge for their service. And they are not trying to recruit the client to their firm. This is just one of their specialties that allows them to create another revenue stream for their business. I suggested to the CPA that this is a resource he may want to bring to Frank's table. If another accounting firm makes the introduction, he could lose the client due to lack of credibility. I made the introduction and the CPA did his vetting. The specialists were brought in and managed to find in excess of $300,000 of tax refunds by implementing some specialty accounting processes. Frank was happy and our CPA's credibility was raised significantly because he brought in talent that has a different perspective. So, the insurance specialist knew an accounting specialist, who could help the client, then connected like-minded (collaborative) accounting professionals, to deliver a big impact for the client and his family. That's how a collaborative team brings unmatched value to affluent clients. Does yours?

Three Shark Tips for your collaborative advisory team:

1. Take Charge of Your Sandbox.
   Invest the money, time and energy necessary to find client-centric advisors who truly like and respect the unique talents of other professionals. Let them know what you expect. Don't pit one against the other. That's no fun and results in people picking up their planning toys and leaving the sandbox. Like leading teams in a company, advisory teams need leadership and direction from the CEO; the client.

2. Hire Advisors Who Share the Sandbox. Confidence is one thing, but arrogance and disrespect have no place on your team. It's natural for an advisor to be invested in a solution that plays to his world view, but openness to other disciplines is paramount. Does your team spend time together, sharing ideas and building trust? Make it happen.
3. Add Some New Sand When Necessary. Did you know that the best sand for making a sandcastle is fine grain, moist sand that holds its shape when squeezed into a ball? Most sand boxes don't have that. You need special sand. It pays to add specialists to your sandbox when you need to hold the structure together. Sometimes that means you have to clear out some old sand to make room for the right stuff. Hire specialists who add value to your planning.

Art Sobczak founded Private Wealth Consultant and co-founded Millennium Insurance Design Group so that trusted advisors could confidently introduce a collaborative life insurance authority to their clients. Art says, "The planning sandbox can be a dirty place. There's a lot of pressure to demonstrate to the client that the fees they are paying are buying excellent value. Some strong personalities can attempt to take over the sandbox. They try to build their sandcastles with only the tools they have on hand. By inviting other advisors into the sandbox, along with their unique tools, a magical transformation takes place. Very quickly a beautiful sandcastle, complete with multiple turrets, a moat, a draw bridge and an escape route takes shape. It looks great. Everyone is happy with the results they've achieved together. That's the magic of collaboration."

Connect with Art by emailing Art@pws-llc.com, or by visiting his website http://pws-llc.com.

BARRY SPENCER &
SCOTT NOBLE

The 3 Reasons Your Financial Success Can Still Leave You With Worries

"Do we have enough?"

A question we hear regularly from successful business owners, executives, and professionals. These are those who have successfully accomplished what 97% of Americans have not: they have accumulated $1 million or more, excluding their primary house (based on SpectremGroup research on affluent in America 2019). Successful; yet, they are still concerned about having enough, even *running out of money.*

If you are concerned, you are not alone.

According to *USA Today*, "Only 13% of Americans with at least $1 million of investable assets feel wealthy... The fear of running out of money in retirement and their reliance on their own savings—rather than Social Security and employer-funded pension during their golden years—make it harder for even well-positioned Americans to feel financially wealthy..." (USA Today "How many Americans with $1 million feel wealthy? Fewer than you may think" July 17, 2019).

There are three reasons that you may not have peace of mind about your money and future.

The first reason is the financial advice industry

Retirement used to sit on a three-legged stool of social security, pension and savings. But not so much any longer.

You are now almost exclusively dependent on the third leg: your savings. The previous generation could count on 80 percent or more of their desired lifestyle covered by social security and a company pension. For most retirees today, that has flip flopped. For most, social security and pension benefits may cover approximately 20 percent of what is needed for a secure lifestyle throughout retirement. Which means that you are now responsible to provide 80 percent of your "retirement lifestyle paycheck," making seasoned advice critical to a lifetime of financial security.

Even among the financially successful who have a financial advisor we have found the fear continues. Like every other industry, the financial advice industry is dominated by some very large companies that not only create and distribute financial products, but also recruit and train "advisors" to sell their products.

The large companies tend to seek to appeal to the masses with one-size-fits-all financial products that they distribute through a large cadre of product salespeople, sometimes calling themselves "financial advisors." This approach can actually work pretty well for people with much less than $1 million dollars, who may not benefit as much from a custom, integrated solution.

The problem occurs when you become financially successful. When you accumulate $1 million, $5 million, $10 million and more, your situation becomes much more complex, your issues become costlier, and the available options become even greater. Success demands a custom, integrated, ongoing solution.

In short, it is our view that many successful people have outgrown the advisor that may have been a good fit when they had less; yet they continue working with them not realizing they have outgrown their advice.

We tend to see this frequently among the people we meet and then serve. Someone is referred to us, or comes to our Private Educational Briefing, or attends one of our Online Educational Events, and we tend to uncover costly errors they were not made aware of, and we show them tax-saving options that they were not offered. And they can become frustrated by not knowing about other possibilities that can enhance their situation.

Their current advisor oftentimes provided appropriate advice when they had less money, but not so much as they increased in financial success. Their financial success can call for an upgrade to their financial advice and benefit from a higher level of skill and more complete planning process. In our experience most successful people are loyal, so making the change is oftentimes difficult on a relational level. However, it can be the key to better preserve, protect and pass on their hard-earned wealth.

Does your current advisor work exclusively with successful people who have accumulated $1 million to $10 million or more? Have they designed and delivered to you a custom, written, integrated lifestyle and legacy wealth plan?

The second reason is the media

Most people forget that the goal of the media is NOT to educate you.

Media's goal is to get you to tune in and pay attention—to read, to listen, or to watch. When more people tune in, ratings go up. Higher ratings mean higher revenue, which is what pays the bills.

In today's information-overloaded world, it's harder and harder to get attention. The most powerful attention-getting tool is FEAR. According to the LA Times, "People pay more attention to negative news than to positive news." The old newspaper adage still remains true, "If it bleeds, it leads." (Los Angeles Times "Why does so much news seem negative? Human attention may be to blame" September 5, 2019).

How is the media making you feel these days about the markets, economy and in turn your financial security?

How much is the media helping you maintain peace of mind?

The third reason is the money myths

Money myths, or financial "wives' tales," have been floating around for years and passed around like truth, making it almost impossible to fully enjoy your hard-earned wealth.

One of the most popular is The Superstar Myth.

How many athletes have been a superstar at two sports? Yet the media suggests that you can master the professional skills needed to create wealth as a business owner, executive or professional; AND, at the same time, master the professional skills needed to successfully navigate all of the financial, tax, and investment issues necessary to preserve, protect and pass on significant wealth. This can lead to unnecessary stress, greater frustration... and can even suck the joy out of having wealth.

The Superstar Myth is usually paired with The DIY Myth. Do-it-yourself (DIY) works on TV, NOT in reality and certainly far less so when it comes to financial preservation.

> *As we finish one of our Tax Reduction and Retirement Income Private Briefings, couples often schedule a complimentary Lifestyle in Retirement Assessment. Quite often, husbands and wives aren't sure they're as well off financially as they originally thought.*
>
> *I usually tell them this: "While you may have been told you are fine, your uncertainty suggests you*

could benefit from our complimentary Lifestyle in Retirement Assessment. It is designed to find out if you are okay. First, by helping you get enhanced clarity about what you want, uncover the dangers that exist in your current plan, and identify the tax saving and lifestyle enhancing opportunities you may be missing. The objective is to give you a clear path for moving forward."

Many couples we see are frustrated, and that's perfectly understandable. Here's what we say to them: "We designed our Lifestyle in Retirement Assessment to be exactly what we would want if we were where you are. It's confidential and it's complimentary. There's no product pitch or portfolio selling. It's our way of giving value first, which is one of our core beliefs. You want to know if you are missing anything. That's why we make our 3-fold promise: One, there will be nothing to buy. Two, I will seek to uncover at least two income enhancing or tax saving opportunities; and Three, you will know what to do next, if anything. Plus, I'll provide you with some additional resources if it makes sense."

When we walk individuals and couples through our 17-Point Lifestyle in Retirement Assessment, we will very often find a number of areas that were either potential financial dangers—gaps that need to be addressed or tax saving opportunities that they want to take advantage of.

As examples, here are a few of the areas we address in the Lifestyle in Retirement Assessment:

1. What tax saving advantages have been created under the new tax laws and are you taking advantage of every option available to you today?

2. How much will income tax rates go up and how vulnerable is your lifestyle in retirement and lifetime financial independence to income tax rate changes?

3. Are you being fully paid for every financial and investment risk you are taking?

Another popular myth is the 80% Retirement Myth. The myth suggests that you can retire on 80% of your final pay. Think about that for a moment. What 20% of your current lifestyle will you stop doing? Aren't there activities, hobbies, etc. that you promised yourself you would be able to do in retirement? Aren't there activities that you want to do more of in retirement? Hobbies? Travel? Visit family and friends? Give more? Eat out? Theater?

To many it can seem ridiculous to think you should "cut back" your lifestyle in retirement. In fact, we believe you should upgrade your lifestyle in retirement.

> *Ideally, the couples we meet with find out with certainty if they really are in good shape. In many cases, they aren't. The couple might be nervous, because they own too much of one spouse's stock from a former employer. They ask, "What happens*

if the company doesn't keep doing well?" They are concerned, because they mistakenly believe they can't get rid of it without paying a ton in taxes.

We find that sometimes couples aren't happy with their current advisor. Maybe, he's a golfing buddy, and they don't know how to extricate themselves from a relationship that isn't working. In some instances, these clients are trying to fill the knowledge gaps they are missing by doing their own financial and tax research. One husband started going to seminars, watching videos and finance shows. He bought a stack of books on investing, stock options, tax planning, and estate planning. It became a second career. After a lifetime of sacrificing to save, the husband become too nervous to spend any money. From what I gathered, the couple had outgrown their current advisor.

I said to them, "There are three things you have right now that you won't always have: money, time and health. I reminded them of the movie, "The Bucket List." I told them: "Imagine being able to enjoy your Bucket List while you have the money, time and health. That requires a lifestyle upgrade—to take advantage of the window of opportunity when you have all three. If you miss that window, you can never get it back. People often come in here after the window has closed, regretting that they missed it."

Here are 3 more of the 17 areas we cover in the Lifestyle in Retirement Assessment:

1. Have you made a Lifestyle and Legacy Bucket List and have a fully funded Bucket List plan?
2. How secure will your money and lifestyle be through the next market downturn and recession?
3. What steps have you taken to neutralize the "hidden taxes" on your IRA and 401k accounts?

The big box financial industry. The fear flaming media. The myths. They are not an objective, tailored, comprehensive plan focused on your priorities and goals and designed to address the dangers you desire to address and the opportunities you seek to take advantage of.

Discover whether you are missing either dangers or opportunities by calling our office at (678) 278-9632 to schedule your 17-Point Lifestyle in Retirement Assessment or go to WealthWithNoRegrets.com for more resources.

Barry H. Spencer is an experienced financial educator, author, speaker, industry thought leader, and philanthropic estate and retirement income planning specialist who you may have seen at some point in *Forbes, Kiplinger, Worth,* affiliates of ABC, CBS, NBC. He is the author and contributor to several books, including *The Secret of Wealth With No Regrets; Giving Transforms You; and Retire Abundantly* and Co-Creator of The Wealth With No Regrets® Process.

Scott M. Noble, CPA/PFS is a seasoned professional education instructor, author, and tax reduction, estate and retirement income planning specialist who is a CPA with Personal Financial Specialist Credentials (PFS). Scott is an author and contributor to *Retire Abundantly* and Co-Creator of The Wealth With No Regrets® Process designed to show business owners, executives and professionals how to save on taxes, have more income and do more of what matters to them.

Disclosures:
Boomfish Wealth Group, LLC, DBA Wealth With No Regrets, is registered as an investment adviser and only transacts business in states where it is properly registered, or is excluded or exempted from registration requirements. Registration does not constitute an endorsement of the firm by securities regulators nor does it indicate that the adviser has attained a particular level of skill or ability. Content should not be viewed as personalized investment advice. All investment strategies have the potential for profit or loss.

Tax, legal, and estate planning information is general in nature. Always consult an attorney or tax professional regarding your specific legal or tax situation. Neither Boomfish Wealth Group, LLC, nor Wealth With No Regrets is engaged in the practice of law or accounting.

MARILYN SUEY

Savvy Women—Taking Control of their Work, their Wealth and their Worth

Start and End each with Gratitude. This mindset will pay long lasting dividends.

·············· TIPS ···············

1. Make a Plan; Take Action
   Your family or individual finances need structure; starting with goals, values, and an honest look at your current and future financial picture. Everyone has a unique story and background that requires custom strategies and tactics. It's never too soon to start planning for your future.

   Plans can be changed and usually do. It's the action taken today that will put you on your unique path in life.

   Start today… done beats perfect every time!

2. Work/Life Integration
   This is a very controversial subject as women have shouldered both "leading" at home and "leading"

at the workplace as well. Despite the Feminist Revolution of the 1970s, many women have found balancing work and family or a personal life, very challenging and frustrating. If we recognize upfront that being Super Woman may not be the answer, then we are half-way home.

Let's live and learn to integrate our choices that best fit our personal dreams and changing life situations.

Emotional intelligence EQ vs. IQ

3. Emotional intelligence, your EQ, is just as important as your IQ. Your ability to be self-aware, self-manage, be socially aware and to manage relationships is a key part of using this critical skill. It does **take practice with intent**, and can be an important factor in your overall success, well- being and happiness as you traverse your own life's journey.

• •

"What Women Really Want and Need…"
7 Keys to Increase Your Financial Fitness, Clarity and Confidence

Women in America have made incredible strides in the past fifty years and the power and influence they hold will only increase in the coming years. A report from BMO Wealth Institute (2015) shared the following data:

- Women are over 51 % of the US workforce and hold 52% of the managerial and professional positions;

- Women are the primary breadwinners in over 40% of America households which is almost a 400% increase since 1960;
- Women are expected to control about $22 trillion of wealth by 2020;
- Women own 30% of private businesses employing over 7.8M workers

And yet current data shows that women earn 79 cents for every dollar a man earns in similar professions. (1) Women are more likely to interrupt their careers to care for families. Although there is reportedly over $1.9 MM families with stay at home dads in 2015. (2)

Women spend as much as 50% more time providing care for aging family members then men.

This care comes at a cost-personally, financially and professionally for women.

In another 2019 study, "Women, Money and Power," from Allianz Life Insurance says that 62% of women feel less financially secure than they did three years ago; (68%) due to lack of confidence in their financial decision-making skills. More than half, 57%, wish they felt more confident.

How do we as women feel more empowered when making every day and long term strategic decisions for ourselves and our families?

What do women really want and what do they need as they take their life's journey?

Let's step back and make sure to address today's social dynamics and demographics for women. We always say that whether you are single, married, divorced, widowed or in a partnership that you should strive to take care of **YOU first**, your financial house, or your financial fitness so that your **money** takes better care of you, starting today, for tomorrow and for life!

Some of you may be your family CFFO, Chief Family Financial officer, and some may be in partnership making these key decisions. Take time to be proactive and take small steps to learn about the critical areas of your financial house. Be part of the decision-making process and do not delegate all the decisions and actions as one day you may be in control of your entire financial house and will want to feel that decision making is comfortable and that you have confidence to make the best decisions for you.

More research has pointed out that women are seeking financial security first, knowing that they can strive for a stable income stream. Most women want their plan to reflect their personal values. While investment performance is important, most women want to know that the overall outcome will support their needs as they take their life's journey. (Strategic Insight Report 2015; Allianz Women, Money, Power Study: Empowered and Underserved 2013)

"Taking Care of your Financial House, So It Takes Care of You"

Case Study 1—Wealth Protection

We worked with two friends and clients who recently moved from California to Ohio and planned to retire there, to be closer to family. Ken was a hard-working successful sales executive in the high technology industry for many years, while Mary was a banking executive, as she raised her family. They had a wonderful lifestyle that they enjoyed with their family and their friends for many years, in northern California, and now in Cincinnati, Ohio.

We had completed a complimentary financial assessment for them about six or seven years ago and designed their Prosperity Blueprint™. During our collaboration we noted that there were a couple of things they may want to tweak and add to their plan to be completely ready for their Second Act (2nd Act) or retirement. These were long term care policies as well as keeping their life insurance in place in case of a premature passing, along with other wealth protection alternatives.

We also advised Ken that he may also want to consider saving more. I said, "If you are thinking about retiring in the next three to five years, you may want to commit to contributing more money to your 401(k) plan now to ensure you can sustain your current lifestyle." They took action on all of our advice and Ken maximized his contributions to his 401(k) plan and kept their life insurance policies in place. Over the past 7-8 years, markets have performed nicely and they were doing quite well after their move to Ohio. Additionally, the cost of living, particularly housing, was much more affordable in Ohio than in California, so that was a large part of their decision to get started on their 2nd Act/retirement lifestyle planning.

Unfortunately, life can hand us unexpected curveballs, and Ken passed away about one year after their move to Ohio, at the young age of 68. The death of a spouse is heartbreaking, however, because of the planning work that we'd discussed, and their quick action, his wife Mary could maintain her lifestyle as she desired. They did take steps to save more, to protect themselves and considered all of their options as they put their Prosperity BluePrint™ into action. Because they did keep their life insurance in place, despite the costs, she has a house today that she owns with no debt and she is living her desired lifestyle with more clarity, increased confidence and financial independence. It could have been a very different picture, if they had not taken action when they could.

We continue to collaborate on Mary's new lifestyle, as an independent woman, making sure she knows with confidence that she has enough money for her lifestyle and her lifetime. Collaborating with Mary, to help her understand that all her investments, her assets, and all the things that she needs to take care of her for the next 30 to 35 years are in place. She made additional decisions to protect herself in case of a critical illness and has a Long Term Care policy and an income strategy for life to provide additional income and wealth protection.

While life can throw you curveballs, designing your customized Prosperity BluePrint ™, you and your family can respond with a strategy that can support you as you enjoy the lifestyle that you desire.

Case Study 2—Managing Your 2nd Act-Your Retirement Lifestyle

Jordan is a senior development officer with a very successful nonprofit and at age 67 decided that she wanted to "retire," and design her 2nd Act. She is an outstanding leader, in excellent health and has two adult daughters. We collaborated on her Prosperity Blueprint™ to see if she was "retirement ready" or not? Jordan had been contemplating retirement for some time and just needed to have a second opinion driven by good old fashioned analyses, data and an ongoing conversation to double-check her feelings about leaving the work place, where she was highly valued by her team and her organization.

Jordan kept excellent records, including budget and cash flow information and she knew her numbers. She knew her lifestyle costs, and had even timed when she was no longer supporting any adult children! That was one of her key factors for her successful retirement plan.

Because she had thought through her purpose and passion, she felt that starting a consulting business in the development arena serving nonprofits would be a good fit for her as her 2nd Act to earn an income and to keep herself busy and engaged.

We worked together intensely for 2-3 months looking at different strategies to build her desired lifestyle post full time employment. She had a comfortable retirement with a pension and Social Security and a health retirement account. For wealth protection she also kept in place a life insurance policy for her family.

Because Jordan could make this decision with confidence and clarity because she had looked deep inside her financial house and built her Prosperity Blueprint™ for her lifestyle, starting today, for tomorrow and for life.

Update, as of June 2019, she is actively consulting, about 15- 20 hours a week and enjoying her lifestyle in her 2nd act with purpose, passion and extra income!

7 Keys to Achieve Financial Fitness, Clarity and Confidence

We contend that your "Wealth is More than Your Money." Wealth includes your family, your friends, your community and the causes you care about deeply. Money is only a tool to take care of you. Making the most of your lifestyle as you plan for your future is key. Let's commit today to making your money work harder for you than the other way around.

1. **Dream bigger and dream bolder!** We like to say," Dream bigger, dream bolder for your brighter future." Aim high in your work, your wealth and your personal worth to be at your highest and best as you take your life's journey.

2. **Plan to reach your bigger dreams.** Start with small steps that will lead you to success. Taking action on your plan will ensure that progress is being made as your see your

future. What you focus your time, energy and passion on will come to you as you work your plan. Reach out and ask for advice and support along the way. Invest in coaching!

3. **Start today!** Design your ideal lifestyle starting today, for tomorrow and for life. We know that "life gets in the way" sometimes. But success is rarely a straight line and most of us may take a path that zigs and zags. As you keep your eye on the "prize," your end goal, results will happen and for your best outcome. We have a mantra that says, "What we appreciate, appreciates."

4. **Understand your numbers!** Let's get serious about "understanding your numbers" in a couple of different ways. One way is to keep tabs on your savings relative to your income at different stages in life. For example, based on a recent study by Fidelity Investments, if you are age 45 and earning $65,000, your savings in retirement or savings accounts should be about 4 times or about $260,000. At age 60, with earnings of $125,000 your overall savings should be about $1MM. Since time is on your side, we recommend that for your long-term savings, leverage the power of compound interest! Or estimate what your lifestyle cash flow needs are in retirement and use this chart to see how much you need to save to retire with confidence.

5. **Know your numbers Part 2!** This is just one way to estimate and assess where you are

in the area of retirement readiness. The other method is to know your lifestyle expenses and design your Prosperity Blueprint™ using both income and expense analyses to refine your lifestyle today, for tomorrow and for the future. Getting comfortable with your lifestyle will make planning easier and give you confidence and clarity as you take steps along the way.

6. **Longevity is no longer rare!** We are living longer! My mother was born during World War I, in 1915, and lived a long and healthy life to age 101! My father, also born in 1915, lived a long and active life to age 91. They both had small pensions and Social Security, plus savings to support their lifestyle comfortably. With healthier lifestyles and modern medical technology, we can all expect to live longer and that means our lifestyle will need to be supported even longer! When FDR proposed Social Security in 1935, the life expectancy of a female worker who retired at age 65 was about 14 years! While the Social Security system is working today it may not be able to support the many millions of younger workers when they are in their retirement years. Regarding when to take Social Security, make an educated guess on maximizing that stream of income. Taking your benefit too early could cost you $100,000 over your lifetime. Take time to look at factors such as health, taxes, and other income sources, as well as spouse or partner situations. Additionally,

with some small exceptions, corporations may no longer provide pensions in retirement. This means that we all must take action to plan for our 2nd or 3rd Act when we no longer work and receive a paycheck. We call this transition moving from paychecks to paychecks. (See notes in Appendix)

Retirement has taken many forms today. Some Baby Boomers have retired comfortably with pensions, social security and savings to enjoy their 2nd Act with no work, perhaps with volunteering for a favorite nonprofit or caring for new grandchildren. Many have started businesses or taken gig jobs to supplement their income post work. And many have found their purpose by following passions that they had and perhaps were not fulfilled during their career.

For the younger generations, stick to the basics of saving at least 10-15% of your income. Use the tax system to your advantage. We will see what Congress does with both Social Security and Medicare in the future which will impact planning for our younger generations.

7. **Protect your wealth!** One of the hidden keys is to have adequate protection as you build and design your ideal lifestyle. Protection may include life insurance for your loved ones in case of unexpected life events. If your employer provides health, life, and disability insurance please make sure to understand your benefits. Life can throw you curveballs and wealth protection like these solutions can be crucial. When possible and

appropriate for you and your family, establish your own protection policies in case you or your spouse loses a job. Take care of you first!

8. **Bonus tip!** One last tip is to provide protection and preservation of your legacy for your family and loved ones. We can share many stories of well-known people who failed to start or complete their planning and it cost their heirs both money and much heartache. For many of us simple wills and trusts can protect and help our families when we pass. For some families there may be more complexities with business entities and assets that may need deeper legal advice. Take action and take care of these money matters.

If you want to learn more about how to take care of your mMoney matters so they take great care of you, download our free e-booklet: **"Retire Happy"** at www.diamondgroupwealthadvisors.com/e-books

For a free consultation on the "Health of Your Financial House" please call or send me an email.

Contact me: Marilyn Suey
The Diamond Group Wealth Advisors
925-219-0080
marilyn.suey@diamondgroupwealthadvisors.com
www.diamondgroupwealthadvisors.com

Marilyn Suey is a registered representative with, and securities offered through LPL Financial, Member FINRA/SIPC. Investment advice is offered through Strategic Wealth Advisors Group, LLC, a registered investment advisor. Strategic Wealth Advisors Group, LLC and The Diamond Group Wealth Advisors are separate entities from LPL Financial. CA Insurance License #0E01981

References

2. Bureau of Labor Statistics household Data Annual averages 2016.

1. AAUW-American Association of University Women- The simple truth about the general pay gap: Spring 2016.

Appendix

Notes
Social Security
www.ssa.gov

Three rules to consider when deciding on your social security benefit:

1. Unless you have very poor health at age 62, try to wait until full retirement age (FRA) or between 67 and 70.

2. If you are married, the spouse earning more should wait until age 69-70, barring health challenges. The spouse who earned less can start benefits FRA.

3. Please ask for advice if you are divorced (married for more than 10 years) or widowed as there are special rules for claiming benefits for you.

You can access Medicare benefit information as well from this site when you are approaching age 65.

The opinions voiced in this material are for general information only and are not intended to provide specific advice or recommendations for any individual.

This material contains only general descriptions and is not a solicitation to sell any insurance product or security, nor is it intended as any financial or tax advice.

Marilyn Suey, MBA, CFP®, AIF™, PPC™ is a nationally recognized **Financial Educator, Author, Speaker and Wealth Planner.**

As the Author of "36 Quick Tips for Savvy Women; Taking Control of Your Work, Your Wealth, and Your Worth" and Creator of *The Personal Prosperity Blueprint™*, Marilyn has been interviewed multiple times, including Leeza Gibbons, **EMMY** *Award* Winning TV and Radio Host; Kevin Harrington, Original Shark on ABC TV's *Shark Tank;* and James Malinchak, featured on ABC TV's Hit Series, *Secret Millionaire*, among others.

As Founder and CEO of The Diamond Group Wealth Advisors, Marilyn and her team have been showing business owners, health care professionals and executives how to preserve, protect and pass on their wealth for almost 20 years. She created The Personal Prosperity Blueprint™ out of her passion to help successful women and men more fully enjoy their hard-earned wealth.

Marilyn is a life-long learner committed to professional excellence. She earned dual degrees in Applied Math and Economics from the University of California at Berkeley; an MBA from the prestigious Wharton School at the University of Pennsylvania; before adding the CERTIFIED FINANCIAL PLANNER™, Accredited Investment Fiduciary™, and Professional Plan Consultant™ professional designations.

It doesn't take long with Marilyn Suey to see why woman and men trust their money and their future to her. She is a warm and passionate communicator who loves to share her financial wisdom and insights as a keynote speaker to many organizations, including Golden Gate University, and to the public through her ongoing seminars, most notably her Savvy Woman Seminar series.

Marilyn shares her leadership skills with many organizations, including as a Board Member with the Senior Services Northern California Foundation, affiliated with Sequoia Living; Blackhawk Country Club; and Advisory for UC Berkeley's, PFP program.

Marilyn lives in Danville, CA with her husband and two daughters. She is a golf enthusiast who enjoys sharing a round with family and friends despite a high handicap. She is a foodie and wine enthusiast and enjoys entertaining and trying new cuisines.

Marilyn Suey is a registered representative with, and securities offered through LPL Financial, Member FINRA/SIPC. Investment advice offered through Strategic Wealth Advisors Group, LLC, a registered investment advisor. Strategic Wealth Advisors Group, LLC. and The Diamond Group Wealth Advisors are separate entities from LPL Financial.CA Insurance License #0E01981

AMY WOLFF

Avoid Divorce Disasters—Choose to Thrive Financially

The secret to getting ahead,
is getting started."
—Mark Twain.

············ TIPS ··············

Amy's 3 Tips to Building Wealth:

1. Be mindful of allowing your emotions to drive your financial decisions.
   - When making important decisions, be sure to do so with enough education and information on the subject. To be good with money, you must operate from a place of controlled emotions.
2. Stop and ask for direction.
   - It is the fastest path to the result you want. Remember to surround yourself with positive, smart people. It will most likely help you be better, get there faster, and have a better result.

3. Invest in yourself.
   - Women are living longer than ever. You are NOT too old to get retraining, pick up a new skill, or to start a business. Bet on yourself. You are your best asset and you are most definitely worth it.

· ·

Avoid Divorce Disasters—
Choose to Thrive Financially.

It is increasingly common to see divorce among spouses ages 50 and older. This has negative consequences for baby boomers' retirement security, according to research from the National Center for Family & Marriage Research at Bowling Green State University. Though the overall U.S. divorce rate has remained steady since 1990, gray divorce—AKA divorce between older couples in long-lasting marriages—has doubled during that period. The report also found the number of baby boomers living in poverty is nearly five times higher among those who are unmarried (19%) than those who are married (4%).

Additionally, statistics from the U.S. Social Security Administration released May 2016, point to the risks of older women who are divorced. The numbers show that unmarried women—including those who are widowed, never married, and yes, divorced—are significantly more likely than men to be poor.

Don't let these statistics get you down. After all, just because statistics exist doesn't mean that *you* have to be one of them. Personally, I am an eternal optimist. Optimism helps me keep my chin up during tough times. And seriously, life is just too valuable to spend it sad, depressed, or angry. I much prefer to focus on living life to the fullest, despite the curveballs that come my way.

Be proactive, take action, and avoid being part of these statistics. My mom did, and so can you.

The journey to get to where I am today hasn't been a short one. In fact, it started over 35 years ago, when I learned that my life was about to change. I was just 12 years old when it happened: I found out that my family was preparing for divorce.

My mom was in her mid-thirties when she divorced. She had been primarily a stay-at-home mom. She married when she was 21 years old, pretty much moving from her parents' house to her first house with my dad. In our home, my dad made the family's financial decisions—so mom had zero experience with money.

As a result of the divorce my mom was awarded the family home. She had her hands full with maintaining the house, paying the bills, running all the errands, carting myself and my two siblings around, and had to manage a full-time job on top of it all. She didn't have anyone to go to for advice, and really didn't have any time to slow down and figure things out. My mom hit some speed bumps and detours along the way. It sure wasn't easy—especially in those early years right after the divorce.

Now don't worry about Mom. She had amazing perseverance, never gave up, and made her way in a man's world. She is financially independent now, but wow, what a tough journey.

I was too young to help mom avoid her financial challenges when she was in the throes of rebuilding. But luckily I am here now to help other women achieve a smoother journey following their divorce.

I was recently giving a workshop to women on finance, and a wonderful woman named Mary came up to me after. Mary, who is in her mid-sixties and preparing to retire, divorced about 10 years ago from a hard-charging spouse who owned a large and successful distribution company.

Mary asked, "I know you have written the book on this, Amy. I've made a lot of mistakes after my divorce and getting to this point wasn't easy for me. I have a best friend who is recently divorced, and I want her to avoid the hassles I went through. If I had it to do all over again, what should I have done differently?"

"Well," I told her, "there are eight major mistakes to avoid in order to help protect and grow your wealth after a divorce. Let's talk about a few of them."

Failing to plan for tax change

Let's get real. Taxes are about as exciting as going to the dentist, right? Most have heard the old adage about how nothing is certain but death and taxes. Unfortunately, it's all too true.

It's pivotal to address tax matters after a divorce. Your financial circumstances have probably changed, as has your filing status. If you don't review and recalibrate, you may have a very big—not to mention unpleasant—surprise at tax time.

Withholding on payroll (W-4)

Immediately after your divorce, review your tax withholding through your employer. You may need to adjust the amount of your income withheld for taxes because:

- Your filing status has changed (from married filing jointly to single or head of household).
- You (or your former spouse) may now be listing your children as dependents.
- You may have a new mortgage on an existing home (refinanced), or you may have a mortgage on a new home.
- Your income may have changed (for example if you moved from part-time to full-time status).
- You may be receiving taxable spousal maintenance.
- You may be taking distributions from your retirement accounts in order to supplement your income.
- You may have repositioned investments to create more investment income.

Quarterly estimated taxes

Unlike wages from an employer, it is not possible to have taxes automatically withheld from spousal maintenance or personal investment income. If you are receiving taxable spousal maintenance or if you have significant investment income, you will probably need to make quarterly estimated tax payments to the IRS for federal taxes and to your state tax department.

On numerous occasions, I have had a new client in my office after filing her first tax return, shocked at the tax bill she just got. Don't let that be you. Take charge, get help, and plan for tax change.

Delaying retitling assets

Reasserting control over your life post-divorce means understanding your financial assets. I mean *truly* understanding what your assets are, where they are, how they're structured, and so on. However, another critical part of re-fashioning your life post-divorce is making sure that you truly "own" all of your assets in both a legal and practical sense.

Re-titling assets simply means that if you were awarded something that was previously held jointly, meaning the asset had both your former spouse's name along with yours, you need to change the ownership accordingly. Similarly, if you were awarded any assets that previously had only your former spouse's name on the account, you also need to re-title those assets in your name. And if the court specified that you receive a certain type of asset post-divorce, such as a portion of your former spouse's company retirement plan, you'll need to follow through to ensure that property is split appropriately.

Why is re-titling your assets so important? Consider some of these common problems:

- I want to sell my car, but both my former spouse's and my name are on the title. Do I really need to track him down to sign off on the title?

- I was awarded my spouse's 401(k) plan. A year has passed, and I am just getting around to completing the Qualified Domestic Relations Order (QDRO) to put the account into my name. However, his company has merged with another company and the account is no longer at the same financial institution. I don't know what to do.

- My portion of my former spouse's Employee Stock Purchase Program has increased substantially, and I want to sell my shares. However, the plan administrators won't let me because the account still has my spouse's name on it.

- I own a mutual fund account that has increased significantly in value and my spouse was awarded a portion of it in our divorce. We both agree that we want to cash in our shares. However, since only my name is on the account, I can make the trade but then I alone will get a 1099 for the taxable gain. How can I fix this?

- My spouse died unexpectedly. We never followed through on re-registering the retirement plan that was supposed to go to me after our divorce. Now the company is saying they need to pay the account over to my former spouse's new wife, who is listed as the beneficiary.

I know when you finally make it through your divorce and reach agreement, you are likely exhausted and just want to get focused back on your children, work, and your own health and wellness. As a result, you may procrastinate—or perhaps you just don't know how to handle the nuts and bolts of post-divorce finance. While many of the problems above have legal remedies, it takes an exhaustive amount of time and money to sort them out.

I can't emphasize this enough. Avoid these problems in the first place by promptly re-titling all of your assets and liabilities.

Not sticking to a budget

Americans in general are not great at budgeting. However, we are pretty good at over-consuming—which is why the average family has $8,000-$12,000 in credit card debt. Yet another roadblock to financial freedom is that when you are suddenly single, the potential to incur additional debt is definitely there. That is, unless you choose to live life differently and become mindful about money.

Bottom line: positive cash flow is the foundation to your financial plan. After a divorce, positive cash flow becomes even more important, as dollars often need to stretch further to support two households instead of just one.

There are five key steps involved in making and sticking to a budget:

1. Understand your income
2. Determine your historical spending
3. Project your future expenses
4. Organize your budget into a cash flow system that will work for you
5. Monitor and update as necessary

Switching to a new cash flow system is hard work and doesn't happen overnight. Think of it as going on a diet or starting an exercise program; it will take a good 30 to 90 days to get into the swing of things and make this a regular part of your lifestyle.

Keep in mind that if you don't consciously develop positive financial habits, you will subconsciously develop bad ones. And if you already had bad financial habits, those habits may become worse.

"This is just the tip of the iceberg," I told Mary. There are 8 areas in total where I commonly see women make big mistakes after a divorce. Email me at amy@ajwfinancial.com to get the full article.

Mary replied, "Any advice for someone who is in the early stages of a divorce? It looks like my younger sister, unfortunately, will need to start down this path."

"Sure. Again, just email me and ask for my article on "5 Tips to Prepare for Divorce."

While I wasn't there for my mom, I'm here now to educate and guide other women, so they make informed and strategic decisions.

You can avoid being part of the poverty statistics. You CAN thrive financially. Just take action and get some help.

Amy's 3 Tips to Building Wealth:

1. Be mindful of allowing your emotions to drive your financial decisions.
   When making important decisions, be sure to do so with enough education and information on the subject. To be good with money, you must operate from a place of controlled emotions.

2. Stop and ask for direction.
   It is the fastest path to the result you want. Remember to surround yourself with positive, smart people. It will most likely help you be better, get there faster, and have a better result.

3. Invest in yourself.
   Women are living longer than ever. You are NOT too old to get retraining, pick up a new skill, or to start a business. Bet on yourself. You are your best asset and you are most definitely worth it.

Amy Jensen Wolff, CFP®, CDFA® is a nationally recognized Financial Educator, Author, Speaker and Wealth Planner for Women and creator of the AJW Thrive Process™. Wolff is the Author of *Ultimate Women's Guide to Thrive after Divorce*. She has appeared in multiple publications, including CNBC and *Star Tribune*, among others.

As a Continuing Education Instructor, CERTIFIED FINANCIAL PLANNER™ and CDFA® (Certified Divorce Financial Analyst®), Wolff shares her unique experience with family law attorneys and other financial advisors.

Wolff is the founder and principal of AJW Financial, a wealth planning firm located in Minneapolis, MN. She and her team guide executive, professional, entrepreneurial and stay-at-home women towards financial independence, while increasing their personal strength and confidence.

Registered representative offering securities and advisory services through Cetera Advisor Networks LLC, Member FINRA/SIPC, a Broker-Dealer and a Registered Investment Advisor. Additional advisory services offered through AdvisorNet Wealth Management. Cetera is under separate ownership from any other named entity. For a comprehensive review of your personal tax situation, always consult with a tax or legal advisor. Neither Cetera Advisor Networks LLC nor any of its representatives may give personal legal or tax advice. All investing involves risk, including the possible loss of principal. There is no assurance that any investment strategy will be successful.

AJW Financial × 3300 Edinborough Way, Suite 550 · Edina, MN 55435 · 952-405-2000

ALAN YANOWITZ

Charity is the Spice of Life

"We make a living by what we get, but we make a life by what we give."
—Winston Churchill

••••••••••••••• **TIPS** •••••••••••••••

1. Improve your life by helping others.
2. Live generously.
3. Live your life below your means.

••••••••••••••••••••••••••••••••••••

"A million dollars! Where will we get a million dollars?" This was Nancy's bewildered response in 1992 when I told her and her husband, Mark, that they would need to accumulate at least one million dollars to reach their retirement goal by her 65th birthday. I had just unveiled their first financial plan, and Nancy appeared overwhelmed. Prior to that day, we had several preliminary meetings to discuss their personal and financial goals. By the time we reviewed my recommendations, their path to success became clearer and they felt ready to implement a plan that could allow them to achieve financial independence.

What is "financial independence?" It's what I call "walk away freedom." Freedom to walk away from the source of your earnings. Freedom to maintain the lifestyle you want. For Nancy and Mark, it meant the freedom to retire from their jobs and live on a paycheck created by their savings and investments.

Mark and Nancy met while attending graduate schools in New York City and married in 1964. Amidst their separate careers, they started a family and finally settled in Cleveland, Ohio, to raise their daughters and son. Nancy worked for a local private college while Mark was the executive director of a non-profit organization. They focused on building their careers and raising their children, but now that Nancy was 50 and Mark was 55, they were thinking about the next chapter of their lives. They wanted to know when they could experience financial independence. And most importantly, they wanted to know if they should be doing anything differently to reach their personal and financial goals.

Before that day in 1992, we also talked about something else...something much more important than their financial goals. We talked about their bigger vision for their future. We talked about what financial independence meant to each of them. Mark shared that it meant spending more time with his children (and future grandchildren). It meant that he would pass on his values and be present in their lives. Nancy shared that it meant giving back to the community by volunteering her time and increasing her financial support to organizations that were important to her. It meant that she could make a positive impact on her community by improving the lives of others.

Most people don't take the time to really think about how they will achieve their vision for their future. They just hope the pieces fall into place and that everything will be okay, but that logic is faulty. It's like going for a ride in your car with no planned destination. Eventually, you'll arrive some place. It might be some place nice, but it might not be. You might be driving for an hour, or maybe all day. You just don't know, and there's nothing worse than arriving at your destination to find that you were totally unprepared for the trip.

Comprehensive planning is like a Global Positioning System (GPS) for your trip. The first step when you use a GPS is to select your destination. You must have an idea of where you want to go. Mark and Nancy had to figure out their destination in order to take the first step in their plan. They knew they wanted to be financially independent within fifteen years. That's when they wanted: walk-away freedom.

The next step was to help them determine their starting point. Just like with a GPS, to find your way you not only have to know your destination, you also need to put in your starting point. Nancy and Mark's starting point was their balance sheet.

Like many people, they had a number of investment accounts at different places that they had accumulated over the years. They had never seen their accounts all together in one place so they could see the total value of their assets. They didn't know how much of their net worth was tied up in their retirement plans, how much was invested in non-retirement accounts, or how much was liquid at any given time. Mark and Nancy each revealed to me they really didn't even know whether they were in the right investments for them.

I assured them that this was not their fault. I explained to them about one of the most common myths today: if you're successful *earning* money and successful *saving* money, then you should automatically be successful *investing* your money appropriately to build wealth. This just isn't so. I further explained that it's analogous to professional athletes. Of the thousands of professional athletes, across dozens of sports, almost everyone has one thing in common: each was successful at the professional level in just one sport. Over the last 50 years, very few athletes have succeeded at, or even attempted more than one professional sport. Similarly, most people don't have more than one profession. And just as athletes have coaches to help them, I was there as their financial coach.

Their plan laid out the steps that could lead to their financial independence. We discussed that just having a plan doesn't create a successful outcome. Nancy and Mark knew the importance of taking action and implemented their plan. It meant increasing their monthly deposits into retirement accounts. They found that they could comfortably tolerate more risk in their portfolio. It also highlighted some potential pitfalls that could derail their plans for the future. One pitfall was the potentially high cost of long-term care.

Rather than self-insure this cost, they chose to transfer some of the risk to their assets with insurance.

Nancy and Mark's plan was not a static document. After that initial meeting, we continued to review and test their plan over the years to mark their progress toward their goals. We met to check whether any changes were needed to keep them on track. If there were, we would make those adjustments. Monitoring a plan is a bit like sailing a boat. In the sailboat, you don't go straight across the water, you tack back and forth. You make corrections to your path based on the direction of the wind. We were making corrections based on their changing goals.

Over time, Mark and Nancy's financial picture changed. Their net worth grew substantially. When we updated their plan in 2009, Mark was working part time and Nancy full-time. Not because they had to, but because they wanted to. They reached their financial goals. **They now had the "walk away freedom" we had talked about in the very beginning!** This would lead to a need to reevaluate their goals and plan we had in place.

Three years later, they were both ready to stop working. Their balance sheet reflected the years of savings as their net worth had grown even higher. They were experiencing what I call the four pillars of an abundant retirement. They were becoming the people they wanted to become. They were in a position where they could do the things they wanted to do. They spent time with the people they wanted to be with, and they were making a difference in their community. Life was pretty good.

They realized what was truly important to them had changed as well. Family became even more important to Nancy and Mark. Their oldest daughter was now married with her own family and living overseas. Their younger daughter was also married with a family and living in Cleveland, as was their single son. They wanted to be sure that their children, grandchildren, and future great-grandchildren would be able to spend time with them and each other both in Cleveland and abroad. Their community became more important to them as well. They wanted to deepen their involvement with, and support of, the causes and organizations that were important to them.

We reviewed their estate plan to see if it was still aligned with what was important to them. Now that they were financially independent, they turned their focus toward their legacy. Even though no federal estate tax would be due when they passed away, I explained that there would still be substantial taxes due at the second death because a large portion of their wealth was in their individual retirement accounts (IRAs). I reminded them that the tax benefits of their retirement accounts had helped them surpass their goals. The first benefit was the tax deduction for each dollar they put in their plans. The second benefit had been the decades of growth without any taxes being paid.

They knew that every dollar distributed from their IRA was 100% taxable as ordinary income. This applied to their children who were the IRA beneficiaries. Thus, as their IRAs grew, so did the tax that their children would have to pay. Nancy and Mark did not want their children to be burdened by this tax. It bothered them that such a large percentage of their IRAs would go to the IRS. It just didn't seem fair to them.

After discussions about how their priorities have changed, Nancy and Mark wanted to plan for the possibility of passing along "a million dollars" to their family as well as to the charities of their choosing. They wanted to know if there were any planning tools that could help reduce the amount of their IRAs that would go to the IRS. We created a model, and with the help of an attorney, implemented a strategy that fit their situation.

Nancy and Mark already had a trust for their children, grandchildren, and future great-grandchildren. Now, they created a new trust that they called a family lifestyle and cohesion trust. This trust could provide funds to pay the expenses associated with overseas travel so that their children and grandchildren could be together for holidays, family visits, and other milestone occasions.

They decided to begin funding these trusts now by redirecting some of their current surplus assets to the trusts. The trusts would jointly purchase a life insurance policy specifically designed for their needs which would provide income and estate tax-free funding for the trusts at their deaths. At the same time, they changed the beneficiary designations on their IRAs so that the money would go to the charitable organizations they were involved with and supported. And since these organizations don't pay income taxes, the entire amount could be used.

At the conclusion of that meeting, Nancy and I reminisced about that conversation at the conference table nearly twenty years earlier. She put her hand on my arm and shared with me that at that time they really didn't know how to move forward and thanked me for helping them create their financial roadmap; a roadmap that not only got them to where they wanted to go but exceeded their vision for the future.

Nancy and Mark were ecstatic about their plan. They derived comfort knowing that there was a dedicated pool of money that would enable their children, grandchildren, and future great-grandchildren to see each other when they wanted. They felt great knowing that upon their passing the causes and organizations that were important to them would also receive such a large donation. Not only would this help their community for years to come, but it would be a legacy for their family. They knew they were passing on more than money as their legacy. They were passing down their values.

My wish for you, the reader, is a journey like Nancy and Mark's. One where you not only reach, but also surpass your goals and are able to leave a meaningful legacy to your family and community.

Note: This story is for educational and entertainment purposes only. The dialogue and people are fictitious and any resemblance to actual people or an actual situation is purely coincidental. There is no assurance that the techniques and strategies referenced will yield positive outcomes. Investing involves risks, including possible loss of principal. None of the information in this document should be considered as tax or legal advice. You should consult your tax advisor for information concerning your individual situation.

Alan Yanowitz, JD is a **Financial Educator**, **Author** and **Wealth Planner**. Alan seeks to show independent women, current and retired executives, professionals and business owners how to help preserve, protect and pass on their wealth and plan for an abundant life. Alan's rigorous legal education and training along with decades of estate and tax planning experience equip him to bring a multi-disciplinary perspective and skill set to help analyze his clients' biggest challenges and implement a custom and comprehensive wealth strategy. Alan has been married to his college sweetheart Dara since 1986 and they have two sons, Josh and Max. He enjoys reading, traveling, and weightlifting. Alan earned a business degree from Northeastern University in 1982 and his Juris Doctorate degree from The Case Western Reserve University School of Law in 1985.

Alan is affiliated with Beacon Financial Partners in Beachwood, OH.

Alan Yanowitz
25825 Science Park Dr., Suite 110
Beachwood, OH 44122

216-910-1864
ayanowitz@beaconplanners.com
www.beaconplanners.com/alan-yanowitz

Advisory services offered through Beacon Financial Advisory, LLC and Capital Analysts, Registered Investment Advisers. Securities offered through Lincoln Investment, Broker/Dealer, Member FINRA/SIPC. www.Lincolninvestment.com. Beacon Financial Advisory, LLC/Beacon Financial Partners and the above firms are independent and non-affiliated. Tax and Legal Services are not offered through, or supervised by, The Lincoln Investment Companies.